The Idiot Boy

Bob Turney

The Idiot Boy Bob Turney

ISBN 978-1-909976-25-2 (Paperback)
ISBN 978-1-908162-96-0 (Epub ebook)
ISBN 978-1-908162-97-7 (Adobe ebook)

Second edition. First edition 2012.

Cataloguing-In-Publication Data A catalogue record for this book can be obtained on request from the British Library.

Cover design © 2015 Waterside Press.
Photography by www.lcthphotography.co.uk. Young boy: Thomas Ward.

Main UK distributor Gardners Books, 1 Whittle Drive, Eastbourne, East Sussex, BN23 6QH. Tel: +44 (0)1323 521777; sales@gardners.com; www.gardners.com

North American distribution Ingram Book Company, One Ingram Blvd, La Vergne, TN 37086, USA. Tel: (+1) 615 793 5000; inquiry@ingramcontent.com

Printed by Lightning Source.

This paperback edition published 2015 by
Waterside Press Ltd.
Sherfield Gables
Sherfield on Loddon   **Telephone** +44(0)1256 882250
Hook, Hampshire   **Email** enquiries@watersidepress.co.uk
United Kingdom RG27 0JG   **Online catalogue** WatersidePress.co.uk

The Idiot Boy

Bob Turney

With a Foreword by Baroness Helena Kennedy QC

WATERSIDE PRESS

"O saints! what is become of him?
Perhaps he's climbed into an oak,
Where he will stay till he is dead;
Or, sadly he has been misled,
And joined the wandering gipsy-folk."

"The Idiot Boy", William Wordsworth, *Lyrical Ballads*, 1798.

Table of Contents

About the author

Since retiring from the Probation Service Bob Turney has pursued a career as an international speaker and author. He makes regular appearances on television and radio and is a guest lecturer in universities and colleges, both in England and abroad. Some of his books are core texts for students of criminology. He is also a gifted and sought after speaker on the after-dinner circuit, at conferences on crime and punishment and motivational seminars—variously described as amusing, thought-provoking, entertaining and truly inspirational. His early life was one of multiple disadvantage, involving dyslexia, drugs, alcohol and crime from which he eventually recovered as described in this book.

The author of the Foreword

Baroness Helena Kennedy of the Shaws QC is one of Britain's most distinguished lawyers. She has spent her professional life giving voice to those who have least power, championing civil liberties and promoting human rights. She has used many public platforms—including the House of Lords, to which she was elevated in 1997—to argue with passion, wit and humanity for social justice. She has also written and broadcast on a wide range of issues, from medical negligence to terrorism to the rights of women and children.

Foreword

Bob Turney is an extraordinary man; yet Bob Turney is also an ordinary man. His back story is sadly all too familiar to many of us who work within the criminal justice system. What is so rare and remarkable about Bob is that, having reached the edge of the abyss, he turned his life around. The lessons for all of us are seminal.

Here was a child whose father had profound mental health problems but no-one considered the impact of a parent's mental illness on a child. When his father finally committed suicide, Bob felt he was in some way responsible; just as children often feel they are the cause of their parents' divorce or a parent's imprisonment or their own abuse. That guilt associated with his father's death pursued him for decades.

Bob was also unable to read or write because, as it eventually transpired, he had serious dyslexia. Labelled an idiot at school, termed educationally subnormal, he was destined for the scrap heap. His self-esteem was non-existent. Like many people with literacy problems, he sought to disguise his failings with disruptive behaviour at school and elsewhere in the years that followed. He made choices throughout early adulthood where his ineptitude would not be exposed. His shame and feelings of inadequacy led to alcohol and drug abuse to deaden the pain, and a life of crime and imprisonment was inevitable.

I could tell you that story, or one very like it, about many people who inhabit our prisons, who become institutionalised and whose recidivism causes untold damage to many, including themselves. These should never be read simply as accounts of personal failure; they point to society's failure and our collective unwillingness to address the underlying problems.

However, Bob Turney's autobiography is an uplifting parable about a life turned around when a human being is treated with dignity and respect. Once Bob was finally given the help he needed and acquired a sense of self-worth and purpose, he came back from the edge. Acts of human kindness changed the course of his life. Love and faith have been his travelling companions on an extraordinary journey of redemption. He has also put his own life's experiences to work in helping other people. I know first-hand the extraordinary work Bob has done with the Probation Service, with Restorative Justice programmes and in his voluntary work with prisoners and young people in trouble. He is an inspirational speaker and motivator; his own life is lived in a way that elicits wonder and awe. Let no-one tell you rehabilitation is not a worthwhile pursuit. It is prison that is the expression of our failure.

Yes, the "idiot boy" is a brilliant man. I feel lucky to know him.

Baroness Helena Kennedy QC
November 2015

Foreword to the First Edition

School days were not the "best days" of Bob Turney's life. Instead they were a time to be endured. School itself was a place where he was labelled, beaten and excluded from lessons. Above all, he was marked out as "educationally subnormal", and as "that idiot boy".

No-one had heard of dyslexia when Bob went to school, and so he would sit at the back of the class, dismissed as being "thick", and be left to look at picture books as his peers went on with their education as best they could. Almost inevitably, Bob later found solace in alcohol and drugs, and then became a prolific burglar to feed his habits. And, again almost inevitably, he would spend years inside Her Majesty's prisons, and in doing so would come to regard them as his second home.

But don't get the impression that *The Idiot Boy* is some memoir of misery, because it is not. It is filled with the hope that comes from having a learning disability recognised and overcome, and triumphs with Bob gaining a degree from Reading University in Forensic Social Work. He would also later work as a probation officer, turning the lives of young offenders around, and using his knowledge and skills to bring some much needed practical experience to add to theories of "youth offending". His is a journey which is truly inspiring.

And we need inspiring stories like Bob's, for research by the Social Exclusion Unit reminds me that 48 percent of prisoners are at or below the level expected of an eleven-year-old in reading, rising to 65 percent in numeracy and 82 percent in writing; and nearly half of all male sentenced prisoners were excluded from school. It is a fact that half of all prisoners do not have the skills required by 96 percent of employers and only one in five are able to complete a job application form.

The message of *The Idiot Boy* is clear—we label and then dismiss young people at our peril, and if only we took greater time, and valued each and every young person there would be less crime, fewer people in prison, and safer communities.

Professor David Wilson

2011

The author of the Foreword to the First Edition

Professor David Wilson is one of the UK's leading criminologists, a National Teaching Fellow and presenter of crime-related TV programmes. Based at Birmingham City University where he is Founding Director of the Centre for Applied Criminology, his books for Waterside Press include *Serial Killers: Hunting Britons and Their Victims 1960-2006* (2007), *Mary Ann Cotton: Britain's First Female Serial Killer* (2013), and *Serial Killers and the Phenomenon of Serial Murder: A Student Textbook* (2015) (with Elizabeth Yardley and Adam Lynes).

To Sue my soul mate, wife and mother of our wonderful five children and grandmother to our grandchildren

The Idiot Boy

Or ... Why I wrote this book and why you should read it!

I do not know how many times that, after a talk, I have been repeatedly told by members of the audience, "You are a 'one off', I feel that my son, daughter or partner will never give up drugs, alcohol or crime as he or she has gone too far down the line." Well, my message is always that no matter how dire things appear, there is always HOPE.

Indeed, the whole point of this book is to let people know that there is HOPE! I believe that by telling my story from the beginning, including the great depths to which I plumbed until I reached the jumping off point and my addictions took me to the edge of life itself, I can illustrate that no matter what that person has done, lost or destroyed there is always HOPE.

There are thousands of people like me, and I have had the privilege of witnessing the miracle of some of their recoveries. I have watched them grow as they move into a whole new way of living; I have seen families reunited, relationships that once were thought to be irreparable, made stronger than they were before.

This book is also for those who have felt hope as their loved ones started to recover and then have had their hopes cruelly dashed as old destructive behaviour has manifested itself again. The pain of watching a loved one slowly commit suicide, emotionally or physically, has no parallel. This book is likewise for those who have had a good upbringing but think "Why am I like this? There's no excuse for me." These people will suffer just as much as they will live with the guilt that they are disappointing their parents, spouses or even children.

This book is for anyone who has ever struggled with a habit or compulsion that has gradually taken over their mental stability or even those who fight every day of their lives to keep negative thoughts or behaviours out of their daily routines. In short, then, it would appear that this book is for everyone! As we get older and supposedly more mature, most of us realise that there will always be areas of our lives that we need to improve. Some habits are less destructive than others, but the principle of changing ourselves and not other people holds. The only talent I have is I can choose a good wife.

I sincerely hope that my story will highlight the pain that those of us with learning difficulties feel as children and often adults. I try to be an example of how determination to face fears, imaginary and otherwise, can bring success in professional and private lives.

Bob Turney
July 2015

Chapter 1

Suicide — a permanent solution to a temporary problem

Anonymous

M y story starts one late afternoon in June 1981. The sunlight shone through the passenger's window of the car I was travelling in, my head bowed, my eyes closed, and my arms folded tightly across my chest in an attempt to stop my hands from shaking. I was rocking myself backwards and forwards.

Beads of perspiration were on my forehead. My head was pounding so much that I felt it was going to explode at any moment, and my stomach was churning with the sensation that I was going to vomit. My right wrist was bandaged to conceal the deep cuts which were a result of an earlier suicide attempt. The mental anguish I was suffering seemed almost unbearable. I just wanted my life to be over, and death would have been a release for me from this mental torment. My death at that time would have gone largely unnoticed by most people: I would have been just another addict who had died in the gutter. I felt a type of loneliness that very few people have known; I had journeyed to the darkest side of life and had reached the jumping off point. I could not struggle any more; I was convinced that life for me was over. This state of anxiety was familiar and had been a part of my life for years. The mental pain and physical discomfort were the result of withdrawal from both alcohol and drugs.

The car slowly made its way through the grounds of Warlingham Park Hospital, a mental institution situated a few miles outside of South London. I was being taken to the hospital for detoxification after twenty years of substance abuse. As we drove through the grounds of the hospital, I lifted my head up; because of the piercing sunlight, I could only slightly open my bloodshot eyes. I could just make out patients walking in the late afternoon sun.

My thoughts flashed back to my childhood in South London. It was a sunny day in the early spring of 1954, and I was nine-years-old. The blooms had just started appearing on the trees. I was walking with my mother up a very long driveway leading to another mental institution. This time we were there to visit my father who had made yet another suicide attempt two months earlier. He had suffered for years with bipolar disorder, and his lifelong struggle with mental illness resulted in many hospitalisations. On several occasions, overwhelmed so much by the grip of deep depression, he would try to end his life.

I had witnessed him take an overdose of sleeping pills, two months before on a cold January evening. At the time my family lived in a two-up, two-down terrace house on the St Heller Council Estate in South London. The family consisted of my father Tom, my mother Winnie, along with my three elder brothers: Tom, Stan and Fred. There was a big age gap between my brothers and me: the youngest, Fred, was eight years older then me. Growing-up they seemed more like distant uncles than brothers; as far back as I can remember they were merely shadowy figures in my life. It wasn't until I hit adulthood that the age gap seemed to close, as only then was I able to form any sort of meaningful relationship with them. As a child, I was closest to Fred. He spent more time at home, whereas Tom and Stan had long since left to go into the army. I have a vague memory of them being at home, all of us sharing the back bedroom and sleeping in one bed. When Tom and Stan left home, it was just Fred and me, sharing the same bed until he got married and moved out.

Due to his illness, my father was unable to work for long periods of time. Money was always scarce and there was never enough coming into the house. We all went without a lot of things: I was mostly dressed in my brother's hand-me-downs, and I remember being sent to school with clothes that were far too big for me. I even had to wear an old pair of my brother's brown plimsolls which were several sizes too big. My mother had to push newspaper into the toes, leaving me to walk around with these old plimsolls flapping about on my feet, attracting a lot of ridicule from the other children in the neighbourhood.

The main source of heating in the house came from a coal fire in the front room; we also lit the oven and gas rings in the kitchen to generate more heat. Despite all this the house was still freezing in the winter months.

Dad had been off work because of his illness for weeks on end, often becoming so depressed that he would stay in bed for days, or sometimes weeks, at a time. It was very cold that winter, so Mum had managed to encourage him to move down to the front room were she made up a bed for him on the settee in front of the blazing coal fire that kept the room warm. He would just lie there staring at the ceiling. On good days, Mum would manage to coax him out and sit him in the armchair by the fire, where he would again spend hours sitting, looking down, and staring at his hands. Some days his depression was so bad that he was in a vegetable-like state, unable to communicate with anyone. Mum would take him in bowls of soup; sometimes she would have to spoon feed him.

On this particular evening, Mum and I were in the kitchen, huddled around the gas oven to keep warm. We would keep out of the front room as much as possible: when in this state of mind my father could only cope for short periods with people around him; when it got too much, he would fly into unpredictable rages and scream at anyone near him. There was also a risk that he could become violent: he had been known on a couple of occasions to assault members of staff in psychiatric hospitals. However, I can't recall any time when he was violent towards us at home; instead, he would vent his anger by smashing up things around the house. We did not have luxuries such as a washing machine, so Mum would boil our clothes in a copper washer on the stove. One morning, my mother was doing the washing and I was having breakfast before school when my father came in and sat at the kitchen table next to me. Then, without warning, he suddenly erupted into a fit of anger, smashing the side of the washer with a rolling pin, and shouting "STOP IT! STOP IT!" at my mother. We later found out that he had been upset by a small amount of steam that was coming out of the steamer.

We could never predict when these outbursts would happen; they would be triggered by insignificant events. Living with him was like having a grenade in the middle of the floor with the pin out, and not knowing when it would explode. As a small child my life was unpredictable; I had to learn to live life a moment at a time.

My mother told me to go into the living room and sit with my father before I went to bed. I entered the room, which was lit only by the coal fire. My father was in bed, staring blankly at the ceiling. He did not move or acknowledge my presence. I walked slowly across the room and sat on the end of the bed with my hands outstretched, warming them by the fire. I sat next to him for a short while; then, without warning, he sat bolt upright in bed, startling me. He had a distant and haunted look in his face. He pointed and said in a flat, emotionless voice, "Get your mother's handbag from the table." It was on the other side of the room. I was completely transfixed. Again he repeated, "Get the handbag" but this time it was much louder with a very menacing tone to it. I picked up the bag and walked slowly towards him, clasping it to my chest. As I got close to him, he suddenly wrenched it from my grip, pushing me to the floor. As I struggled to my feet — to my horror — I saw him reaching for a box of sleeping pills which my mother must have put in her bag for safekeeping. With the speed of light, the lid was off and he had crammed the entire contents into his mouth. Some tablets spilled through his fingers and fell onto the bed; he scooped them up with his other hand and continued pushing them into his mouth. The whole episode was over in seconds.

Again, I stood transfixed, frozen to the floor and unable to move. Having heard my fall, my mother came to investigate and broke the spell. When she realized what had happened, she shouted, "Tom what have you done?" Then she turned to me and said, "Why did you give him my handbag, you idiot?" I ran from the room with tears rolling down my cheeks. I ran upstairs to the bedroom searching for my teddy bear, "Mickey". I had come to depend on him more and more for comfort each time Dad was taken ill. I crawled under the covers, sobbing my heart out. Not only had my father tried to kill himself, but I had aided and abetted him in doing so. The pains of guilt washed over me in the dark and cold room.

There was a lot of commotion going on downstairs. Mother had summoned the neighbours for help. One of them went to the telephone box to call the doctor; the other was trying to comfort my mother and help my father. I am not sure how long I laid awake in that darkened room before I fell asleep. I had heard the doctor come and could hear a lot of muffled conversations going on before an ambulance arrived to take my father away. Soon after, I was asleep.

The following morning I was told nothing except that my father was in the hospital. I was given some breakfast then ushered out the door. I was told to go to school; I could only assume that my father was still alive. I left for school with my mind still in a state of turmoil. I was so confused; the burdens of guilt hung heavily on my shoulders. There was no-one in whom I could confide. The other kids would tell the teachers about the things they had done with their parents; how could I tell them that last night I had helped my father make an attempt on his life?

My family never discussed my father's mental condition with me; they must have felt that I was far too young or ignorant to comprehend what was going on. For me, the most painful part was that no-one acknowledged my feelings. If they had, maybe I could have expressed the overwhelming, misplaced guilt I felt about the whole episode. Maybe if I could have received some reassurance that it was not my fault my father was in hospital again, perhaps this would have gone a long way towards dispelling the enormous sense of guilt I felt.

The only information about my father's condition I received was from the other children in our neighbourhood, whose parents had been telling them half-truths. A lot of parents would tell their children to keep away from me. There was a lot of ignorance about mental illness in those days; people genuinely felt that my father's mental condition was contagious. As far as they were concerned, their kids should keep away from me; we had the reputation of being the family of a madman. It was only in later years that I managed to find out from my brothers the sort of treatment my dad received in hospital. He would have to undergo electric shock treatment for his depression, where an electrical current was passed through his brain resulting in an epileptic fit. In those days there were no such things as muscle relaxants. It was a barbaric way of treating depression. My father would drift in-and-out of a coma for days on end; I was only allowed to visit him in hospital when he was in a more presentable state.

As I walked up the driveway of the hospital with my mother in that early spring of 1954, I had a heavy heart. Here was a nine-year-old boy convinced in the back of his mind that he was responsible for his dad being in hospital. As I had not been told anything about his condition, I just imagined that he would be on some sort of life support machine. To my great relief he was in the grounds, fully dressed to meet us.

About a week after that visit, Dad was discharged from hospital. When he came home there seemed to be a change in his behaviour. Whatever they did to him it seemed to work: he was more stable than he had been for years. He was able to work, able to pop down the pub for a swift half. Life seemed to be on the up for us. Sometimes luck seemed to smile down on our family. In the early summer of 1954 my father won £90 on the football pools, the equivalent of almost six months' salary for him. My parents fitted me out in new clothes and shoes. When I dressed myself, I felt that I was on top of the world. We never had family holidays: the money was simply not there for such luxuries. However, father's winnings seemed like a fortune to my parents, so my dad announced that we would go to Brighton on the upcoming Spring Bank Holiday.

When the day arrived, I got up early, dressed myself in my new clothes, and joined my parents who were in the kitchen preparing egg and cress sandwiches for our train journey. The whole day was wonderful; the sun was shining; both Mum and Dad were in good moods, chatting happily to each other, which was not a regular occurrence. We boarded the train for Brighton. As it made its way through the countryside, I sat gazing out of the window. I had not seen much of the rural part of the country; I had scarcely been very far from South London. The only time I had a chance to get a brief glimpse of the countryside was from the top of a Green Line bus when I was visiting my father in mental hospitals just outside London. Today was different. Mile after mile rolled past my window. My concentration was only broken by my mother giving me a sandwich.

As the train pulled into Brighton, the excitement mounted because shortly I would be seeing the sea for the first time. As we walked down the hill from the station, there it was stretching out in front of us. It was the most breathtaking sight I had ever seen. It felt so good to have the sea air flowing into my nostrils and filling my lungs. I was so excited. It was a wonderful day: the sun was warm; my mother sat in a deckchair; my father played with me. At lunch time, we had fish and chips, and in the afternoon we went for a walk around the town. We passed the Grand Hotel and Dad told me that people had to be very rich to stay there. I felt like a millionaire myself that day. On the way back to catch the train home we stopped off at a gift shop where I fell in love with a cricket bat. To my great joy, Dad brought it for me. It was the most wonderful day of my life; we did not seem to have a care in the world. On the journey home I fell asleep in my father's arms, a perfect end to what had been a perfect day.

After that, his health began to decline to a point from which he never recovered. He was becoming more and more obsessed with death. At one stage, he got involved with the local Spiritualist Church. He was desperate to find out what would happen to us after we died. He would visit mediums who would conduct séances. He would come home from church and tell me stories of manifestations of spirits — as he would call it — from the afterlife. I increasingly hated being on my own and became terrified of the dark.

Dad's life followed the same familiar pattern of violent mood swings. Some days he would rush about maniacally. It would appear that he did not have a care in the world; he was fun to be around. This period was always followed by days when he plunged into a deep depression and would not talk to anyone. He would just sit in the armchair staring at his hands, or he would start to play sombre music on the piano. Then there would be outbursts of anger. As my mum and I were often the only ones at home, we bore the brunt of Dad's illness. My brother Fred was rarely at home. He would spend a lot of his time out socialising with his friends, most of the time either drinking down the pub or betting at the dog track. I longed for Fred to come home.

He had a wonderful sense of humour and was blessed to always see the funny side of life. Fred was an oasis in the desert of my uncertain life. For me, the only thing in life that was certain was uncertainty. Somehow he took me away from that sad life I was leading. It seemed that my father's illness had a stranglehold on me at times, but Fred would arrive home like the cavalry and transport me away from that depressive home life and surround me with laughter.

Friday 13th August 1954: the day I'll never forget. Dad was in bed; I was about to go the shops with Mum. I put my head around the bedroom door to say goodbye to him, and told him that we were just popping to the shops. He made no reply. As we returned to the house, a strange still-ness hung over the place and a morbid sense of foreboding greeted us at the front door. The house was deadly silent. I ran up stairs into the bedroom to discover him bent over, half in the bed. His face was ghostly white: he was dead. It was only later we found out that he had drunk a fatal dose of weed killer. I stood there emotionless for what seemed like an eternity, staring at him. It was only a matter of seconds before Mum was in the room. She told me to go and get help from next door and then keep out of the way. I went out and knocked on our neighbour's door, told the women that Dad was dead and that Mum needed some help.

When I went back into our house, Mum was now at the bottom of the stairs. She told me to go and find a friend to play with. I tried to blot out my emotions by going into denial and refusing to believe what was happening. I conjured up a world of make-believe, hoping that I would be safe. For me this was the coping mechanism I used so that I did not have to face up to what I had just witnessed. I started to play football in the road near my house with a friend. Not long afterwards, an ambulance arrived. Two men rushed into the house; it seemed like hours later that they finally reappeared with Dad's body on a stretcher. People were standing at their front doors, watching. When the ambulance pulled away they all went inside, closing their doors and leaving me in an empty street. We watched it disappear at the end of the road. The mother of the boy I was playing with came and ushered him away; her body language and tone of voice told me that she did not want her son to have anything to do with me. So I was left standing, alone, in the street.

It was one thing for my father to continually be going in-and-out of mental institutions, but it was another thing entirely for him to try and kill himself, and to succeed in the end. Unlike politics or religion, suicide is not a topic of conversation. The very thought of someone choosing to take their own life can often leave people with a profound sense of bewilderment; it can challenge their deeply held beliefs about life and death.

By late afternoon, rumours of my father's suicide had started to fly around. I picked up the vibes from other parents who lived in our neighbourhood that they did not want their children to associate with me. I spent most of the day out in the street looking for the company of other children, but there seemed to be no-one around. From that moment on I felt so alone.

Tom and Stan, my brothers, were contacted and had been granted compassionate leave from the army. Tom's wife came to look after me while my mother had to deal with the police and their investigation. Fred had been contacted at work and he had gone straightaway to help comfort our mum. When someone in the family chooses to take their own life, there is an emotional minefield left behind. I had an overwhelming feeling of guilt and had questions like, "What did I do to make him want to kill himself? If I had not gone to the shops that morning maybe I could have stopped him from doing what he did?" My dad's death left me with loads of emotions: there was guilt, but most of all there was anger. How could he have done that knowing that I would find him? He must have hated me to do that to me.

My family felt that it would be in my best interests if I did not attend the funeral. It was arranged that a friend of the family, a delivery man, would look after me and I would go with him while he was doing his rounds. When the morning of the funeral arrived, my family carried on as normal, trying desperately to shield me from what was really happening. When the man called for me and I was safely out of the way, they must have frantically rushed around the house getting dressed for the funeral. The man had his son with him and all three of us made our way to his work. As children were not allowed in the yard, the two of us had to wait outside while his lorry was being loaded.

There was a long delay in the loading, and we were forced to sit outside much longer than anticipated. It was there, sitting by the roadside, that I saw my father's funeral procession pass right by. I was only a few yards away from my family, but it might as well have been a million miles. The moment I realised what was happening, I rose to my feet. If I had been just two yards nearer, I could have reached out and touched them. It only took a few moments for the cars to pass me; however, it seemed like an eternity as I stood there. I raised my hand in a gesture of acknowledgement to my family; they saw me but did not acknowledge me. As the hearse passed with my family in the following car, I stood there with my hand held up slightly and my stare fixed on the procession. I was in some sort of surreal world and I could not believe what was happening. I felt like an outcast and that my feelings were unimportant. I had no closure to my dad's life because I was not allowed to attend his funeral.

I'm sure that my family meant well; in their own way, I believe that they were tying to protect me. However, getting no emotional response from them came across to me as indifference. If someone shows you anger or love, they are both emotions that say they recognise you as a human being; but indifference — that's when you're not acknowledged as a person.

Chapter 2

I have never let my schooling
interfere with my education

Mark Twain

School turned out to be a nightmare. I'm profoundly dyslexic and have got the reading age of an eight-year-old. My spelling is so bad that whenever I use the spell check on my computer it always wants to know what language I am writing in! When I was at university they wouldn't allow me to have lunch breaks because it would cost too much to retrain me when I came back!

The condition went undiagnosed until I was in my late thirties, and today I am registered as disabled with it. Being a dyslexic author is like being a blind darts player; however, with a good computer, a great proof reader, and an editor with an excellent sense of humour, I manage to write books.

There are many different types of dyslexia; my type is dyseidetic, which means that the brain does not correctly process the images that are transmitted to it. As a result I have a problem with reading things properly: my brain leaves out words or adds ones which are not there. Consequently, much of what I read makes little or no sense to me. Let me give you a simple example: "The dog bit Johnny" is a straightforward sentence; however, I might read it as "Johnny bit the dog". The whole meaning of the sentence is thrown out of the window. When I read, I have to take it very slowly; I might have to reread something several times before it makes any sense to me. My eyes will always move around the page very fast—which is so tiring—and I can only read for short periods at a time before I have to rest.

I also suffer from dysphonetic dyslexia, which means that my brain does not correctly process the sounds that I hear. As a result, I am not able to pronounce words correctly, or I will use the wrong one. I mix up words, so it sounds like I have a speech impediment; as a public speaker, this can also make life a little bit difficult for me. Growing-up, my family and teachers were constantly correcting the way I spoke. They would say things like, "For goodness' sake, don't be so lazy and pronounce your words properly." That would only put me under pressure; my pronunciation would become even worse, and their criticism would increase. It was a vicious circle.

One morning, when I was working as a probation officer, I phoned my secretary to tell her that my wife was unwell and so I was going to be slightly late as I needed to sort the kids out before I was able to come in to work. I asked her to please apologise on my behalf to any people I had appointments with, and to reschedule them. Once I got the kids sorted, I made my way into the office. My secretary asked me, "What's wrong with Sue?"

I said, "She has meningitis!" I was then asked, "Is she in hospital?" "Oh, no, she'll be up and about in a day or two once the antibiotics have kicked in. She'll be fine." That was my response; however, not happy with my answer, my secretary went about trying to shed some light on what I was trying to say. What I meant to have said was that my wife had "laryngitis"! As you can see, when I'm talking to some people they can often end up with puzzled expressions on their faces. I also lack any sense of coordination and have great difficulty telling the difference between my left and right. This leads to all sorts of problems, especially if I'm asked to give someone directions.

Shortly before Dad's death, my mum took me to a speech therapist which did help a bit; however, when Dad's health went into decline, she stopped. At primary school, I was sat at the back of the class with a big picture book to look at because I was unable to grasp what was going on: they might as well have been teaching in Chinese as far as I was concerned. I didn't have a clue.

Mum was too preoccupied with trying to keep Dad alive to notice my underachieving at school. When she got my school reports stating that they believed I was of "simple mind", she and the family believed it. I turned eleven a year after Dad died, and was due to take the eleven plus exam. Depending on how I preformed it would decide whether I went to a grammar school or a secondary modern. The school wrote to my mum inviting her in to discuss my future education. They told her that I had no chance of passing the exam, and that they were going to put me straight into the secondary modern: in their opinion I was an "educational subnormal". She was told not to expect anything from me, and that my future employment prospects were nil. They went on to say that they believed I was bordering on being mentally-retarded.

Mum never questioned their opinion, even though there had never been any psychiatric assessment carried out on me. To be fair to her, in those days there were several people you just didn't question: bank managers, doctors, and school teachers being among them.

By now my brother Fred had been called up for National Service, and so it was just me and Mum at home. When I would go to bed at night, all I had to hold on to was my teddy bear, Mickey. I would pull him close to my face; his smell was so comforting. He had changed quite a bit since I first had him as a baby: some of his stuffing had come out and Mum had stitched him up a few times; he had lost an eye; and he had some bald patches where his fur had fallen out. Nonetheless, he was the only stable thing in my whole life. I was missing Fred, so Mickey was playing an important role. Such things always do in the lives of children. In recent years, it has been a pleasure to give the father of the bride speeches at my daughters' weddings. We have always held on to their teddies or their comfort blankets, and I would produce them as a visual aid during the speeches. Both my girls and my son-in-laws have loved it; it never fails to bring back memories.

By now Mum had got a full-time job working in a local factory; she would leave for work early in the morning and not return until six in the evening, leaving me to fend for myself. The job represented a whole new freedom for her: for years she had nursed my dad; now she was free to come and go as she pleased. She found friends at work, and had a regular income, which was, of course, her prime motivation for working. It may not have been much, but it was enough for us to live on.

I didn't have many friends, but one family who lived near to us took me under their wing: Frank and Queenie Bradford. They had four kids: the eldest was Thelma, then there was Mickey—we became lifelong friends—then twin boys, John and Phillip. They were the typical South London family—salt of the earth. Queenie very much ruled the roost. She had a great capacity to love her children, and I could always find a meal at her house. Years later, when the police were after me, they went to Queenie's looking for me. She gave them a volley of verbal abuse on the doorstep and refused to allow them in to search the house for me without a warrant. I was hiding in her garden shed.

During the summer holiday, my mother would go off to work at seven thirty in the morning, leaving me asleep in bed. She made sure that there was some food in the house and sometimes would leave a small amount of money for me. As I had few friends in the neighbourhood, I spent most of that holiday at the Bradford's.

That summer I was consumed with fear: in the autumn I was to start my new school. Soon the dreaded day arrived. As usual, my mother woke me up before going off to work. Even though it was years ago, I still remember the feeling of fear I had on that morning, getting ready to go to school in an empty house, being too nervous to eat the breakfast that my mother had left for me. I started the mile walk to school with butterflies in my stomach. That feeling of impending doom had been with me throughout the summer break; now it was magnified one hundred percent to a point where I felt physical pain.

When I arrived at the school gates, I stood frozen to the spot, not wanting to go in. Other new kids walked past with one or both of their parents. I stood there gazing through the gates, watching the other children filing in; eventually, I summoned enough courage to walk in, finding a solitary corner of the playground to stand while waves of fear washed over me. One of the teachers, who was to be my form master, came into the playground, blew a whistle, and told all the new boys to form a line to his left. I later learned that his name was Mr Johnson. He was a young man in his mid-to-late-thirties; he always wore white plimsolls, a navy blue blazer and grey flannel trousers. He was a physical education teacher, hence the plimsolls. During the war, he had served as a rear-gunner in the Royal Air Force, and would hold us all transfixed with stories about the bombing missions he flew over Germany.

It was not long before I was to fall foul of a particular teacher named Mr Williams, who taught English. He was Welsh — there's a paradox in a Welshman teaching English! He also taught history, and was one of the most feared teachers in the school. Like Mr Johnson, he was also in his mid thirties, tall, with a large nose and a full head of hair. He always wore a sports jacket with leather patches on the elbows, a brown pair of trousers with a shiny seat, and a pair of highly polished brown shoes. He drove an American ex-army jeep.

Within a couple of weeks I found out just how cruel he could be. Due to my learning difficulties, he would make me sit at the desk nearest to his table. He claimed that it was the best way he could keep his eye on me. In his English classes, he would ask me to spell a word he knew full well that I couldn't spell. I would not even make an attempt to spell the words; I would just sit at my desk with my mouth half-open, glued to my seat with fear. He would then stand up from behind his table and move quickly to where I was sitting. He would say, "Come here, Idiot Boy!" He named me after the Wordsworth poem, "The Idiot Boy". I cannot remember him calling me anything other than that. He would grab me by the short hair on the side of my head and pull me out from my desk, dragging me to the front of the class. Still holding me by my hair, he would ask me again to spell the word. When I couldn't, he would start to beat me with his free hand on the back of my head as he spelled out the word, bringing mocking jeers from the other boys in the class. When he had finished, he would push me back into my chair.

There were times when each boy in the class would read something from a book. When it was my turn, he would preface the event by saying, "Now, let us hear from the Idiot Boy." I was so fearful I could not get a word past my lips. This was swiftly followed by yet another beating from Williams and taunting from the rest of my classmates. I learned to quietly accept the abuse and ridicule; any motivation I had to learn had long ago left me.

In the playground most children made fun of me. I had few friends, apart from Mickey Bradford and a couple of his friends. My time at school was extremely lonely. I desperately wanted to belong and would do anything to be accepted by the other kids; this sense of wanting to belong remained with me for years. I had no sense of my own identity and became what is known as a "people pleaser". I would always agree with what was being said, which left me very vulnerable to negative behaviour. Thinking back to those times, it's difficult to believe that years later I would not only hold my own, but win a debate on law and order at — of all places — the Oxford Union!

The rest of the teachers were not a great deal better than Williams. Some were alright, but by and large I was treated as some sort of simpleton. However, there was one who matched Williams. Mr. Parry was in his mid-to-late-forties and was overweight, balding and had a glass eye. He taught metalwork. Due to my lack of co-ordination, I would often make mistakes, causing him to grab me by the chin with his thumb and forefinger in a vice like grip, lift me up on my tiptoes, hit me on the back of the head, and call me a clumsy idiot.

If there was a competition between the two of them as to who was the most savage, I would have said it was a dead heat. Both would beat me with the cane at the drop of a hat, and both took great joy in calling me an "idiot". I told my mother about the abuse, but she was reluctant to do anything about it: she believed that you did not question professional people. I continued to badger her and she eventually made an appointment with the teachers. However, the abuse was denied; instead, she was told about my refusal to engage in schoolwork. She became more concerned about me making up stories than about my treatment at school. She would accuse me of lying, and so I stopped complaining and suffered the abuse in silence.

Things went from bad to worse at school and I just tried to survive in the classroom by disengaging mentally during lessons. My thoughts would only be broken by Williams, who continued asking me to spell words which I could not. This would be followed by the obligatory humiliation and beating.

School became impossible; I could not concentrate on anything, and fell even further behind with my work. One time, after a particularly bad day at school, I came home and went to my room to find my teddy bear, Mickey. He was missing. I searched the house but he was nowhere to be found. I waited for what seemed like a lifetime for my mum to return home from work and asked her if she knew where Mickey was. She told me I was too old to have teddy bears, and that it was ridiculous that a boy my age would have such a thing; it was about time that I grew up, and I should start by acting in a more responsible way and that meant not playing with teddy bears. She said that she had come home during her lunch break and had thrown him away. I could not believe it. Mickey had been my comforter, particularly during the times that I had been so frightened; I had buried my face into his soft furry body which had soaked up my tears. Now he was gone! I was totally devastated. If this is what it meant to be more "grown up", then I did not want any part of it.

The playground was a minefield. If Mickey Bradford was about I would mix with him, which would keep the bullies away. There was a day then he wasn't at school, and so I was picked on by the school bully, Alex Cuttings. I was standing in the corner of the playground on my own; he came over to me with a few of his friends and asked if I had a cigarette. When I told him that I didn't have any, he became angry, put both hands on my chest, pushed me backwards and said, "I'm going to beat you up after school, Turney!" As he started to walk away with his friends, having thrown down the gauntlet, something snapped inside of me: I knew that I couldn't do much about the teachers bullying me, but I wasn't going to let him get away with it. I called after him,

"You can try!" He laughed at me and said, "You're dead, Turney. I'll see you after school."

I felt physically sick; I was shaking inside; I didn't know which way to turn. How was I going get out of this one? If I didn't turn up for the fight, my life would be hell, and I just couldn't take any more of the bullying. I thought the best thing that I could do was just turn up and take a beating; at least I would go down fighting.

That afternoon, the rumours were running riot around the school about the fight. I was feeling sick. The school bell rang for the end the day, and as I walked out of school all of the Cuttings supporters around me were jeering, shouting out things like, "You're dead, Turney". I tried to shut them out of my mind as I walked to the piece of waste ground were the fight was to take place. I was shaking like a leaf. I remembered that my brother Tom was in his school boxing team and had shown me some tricks.

When I got to the waste ground, most of the school was there. The crowd opened-up, and in the middle stood Cuttings, who was a bit bigger than me. The crowd closed in around us; they were chanting "Fight! Fight!" He made a rush at me, his arm out and head down, charging at me like a bull. His intentions were to grab me around the waist and wrestle me to the ground, beating me when I was down. As he got near to me, I side-stepped him and threw a right punch, hitting him square in the jaw. He fell to the ground. As he got up, he said, "I want to wrestle you!" I said, "Tough," then stepped forward and delivered two right hooks to his face, followed by a left hand to the stomach, sending him to the ground again. The crowed went mad; I screamed at him to get-up. Something inside of me had snapped: I felt a rush of anger go through my body. It was a release of all the frustration I had felt up until then, a surge of energy. I can only liken it to the rush amphetamine gave when I first took it. It felt so liberating.

He wasn't getting up. I rushed over to him, picked him up by his shirt, and started raining down punches on him with my right hand. The blood started to appear from his mouth; I landed a heavy right to his nose, which started to bleed. With tears in his eyes, he said, "No more please!" He got up and started running in the direction of his home.

I stood there for a moment. Some of the crowd were patting me on the back. For the first time in my life I had achieved something: I had beaten up the school bully.

The following morning at school, Mickey Bradford congratulated me, and again the rumours were flying around the school. Cuttings wasn't in school and rumour had it that he was in hospital. It wasn't true, but it all added to my street cred. By about mid-morning, his mother went to see the headmaster. She was complaining that her son had been beaten up by bullies, but she didn't know who had done it and was threatening to call the police if the people responsible didn't own up. Nobody did.

The following day Cuttings returned to school. He had two black eyes, his nose had been broken, and his top lip swollen. I was walking down the school corridor with Mickey when Cuttings walked pass. He didn't look at me. On seeing the facial damage, Mickey turned to me and said, "Nice one, Bobby boy!", and started to laugh.

From that time on, other boys who hadn't given me the time of day before were now speaking to me. My fight with Cuttings had upped me in the popularity stakes. A couple of days later, a prefect told me that I had to report to Mr Johnson, the games master, after school. As he was also my form master, I was convinced that he was going to ridicule me over my written work.

The school bell went for the end of the day, and I made my way to his classroom feeling very nervous. I knocked on the door. I stood for what seemed ages, but it was only a moment before he called out, "Come in."

I walked in; he was sitting at his desk marking some exercise books. He didn't look up as I entered the room; he just stretched out his right hand to indicate that he wanted me to stand in front of his desk. Once again it seemed like ages, standing there, before he lifted up his head he said, "Well, Turney, what have you and Cuttings been up to?" Leaning back in his chair and crossing his arms, he looked up at me. "Well, what have you been doing?"

"Don't know what you mean, sir!"

"Come on, Turney, I wasn't born yesterday. You know what I mean."

"Sir?" I said.

"Cuttings didn't get those black eyes and broken nose playing tiddlywinks, did he?"

"Nothing to do with me, sir."

"Turney, don't take me for a fool; I've got my ear to the ground. When someone farts in this school, I know about it. What do you think we have prefects for?"

"I still don't know what you're talking about, sir."

"Look, I know that you gave Cuttings a good hiding a couple days ago, and it wasn't before time: he had been asking for it. I know it was you, and by all accounts you did a pretty good job on him. I was told that he didn't lay a finger on you. Well done, son!"

We both smiled at each other. "Now, the reason why I called you in is because I'm putting the school boxing team together for this year's All England Schoolboy Championships, and I'm short of someone in the bantamweight class. I feel you can fill that class for me."

"Me, sir?"

"Yes you, sir. We start training next week. I've had a word with Mr Williams and he has agreed to let you off his English class so that you can start training with the team."

"But I've never boxed before!"

"Well, going by what happened a couple of days ago, you gave a good account of yourself, anyway. Didn't I read somewhere that your elder brother Tom was in the school boxing team? I'm sure he will be able to give you some good tips."

As I left the classroom, I wasn't sure what I had let myself in for; I was just relieved about getting time off from English classes — now that was good news! But how was I going to cope in the boxing ring?

Chapter 3

First we make our habits, then our habits make us

Anonymous

By now my brother Tom had been demobbed from the army and was living in Tooting with his wife and baby daughter. I told him what happened at school and that I had been selected for the boxing team. He began to show me some of the finer points of the sport.

Both Fred and Tom had friends who were boxers. Living down our street were two brothers, Terry and Ronnie Lake, who had both turned professional and were doing well. Around the corner lived Don Cockell's parents. Don fought Rocky Marciano for the World Heavyweight title in 1955; I remembered it well as it was just before Fred was called up for National Service. With Don being a local boy, my neighbourhood was buzzing with excitement; everyone was talking about the fight for days before. It took place in San Francisco and was broadcast on the radio at about three in the morning. Fred got me out of bed and we went downstairs to listen. The reception was poor, the radio was crackling, but the flight was classic toe-to-toe stuff. The referee stopped it in the ninth round because Don was getting a terrible beating. However, to his credit, he lasted much longer than anyone expected — all the pundits had predicted that he wouldn't last more than three rounds.

Going nine rounds with Marciano was no mean feat, considering he retired undefeated, a record that even the great Muhammad Ali couldn't beat. It was about a week after the fight when I ran into Don outside his parents' home. To a ten-year-old boy he seemed like a giant of a man. He was wearing sunglasses because of the eye damage he had suffered in the fight, and was carrying two small Pekinese dogs. It seemed strange to me that here was this heavyweight boxer with two small dogs in his hands — which were almost as big as the dogs! — and yet he was very gentle with them. He smiled and said, "Hello," then put the dogs in his car and drove-off.

Some years later, Don and I became drinking partners. He would sit on a stool at the end of the bar reminiscing about the glory days. He had a great sense of humour and could have made a fine after-dinner speaker or sporting pundit, or had his own column on the back pages of a national newspaper. Unfortunately for Don, there was no life after boxing: his fortunes took a nosedive and he died penniless. By contrast, Henry Cooper, another heavyweight boxer and a contemporary of Don, became a national treasure. He successfully reinvented himself, and "Our Henry" was knighted in 2000. He died in 2011 a true legend

A couple of years ago, Mickey Bradford organized a school reunion. Many of these people I hadn't seen for over thirty years. Some had done well for themselves and had great families and jobs. However, there were others who kept harping back: they would say things like, "Do you remember when I did this?" — things I couldn't even recall. I kept thinking to myself that I had done a million things since then. Even though I kept asking what they were doing now, all they wanted to do was talk about the past. They hadn't moved on; they seemed discontented with their lives; they preferred to stay in the past. That was what Don was like: he was happier living in the past; he didn't want to move outside his comfort zone.

Training had started for the school boxing team on Tuesday and Thursday afternoons, when I should have been in my English class. I got the great delight of running around the playground when the rest of the class were in their lessons. It was a respite for me from the Welsh maniac, which was great, but I'm sure the feeling was mutual. He must have been pleased to see the back of me: he had long since given up on me as a no-hoper.

Each training session lasted two hours, one hour in school time, and the other after school. The rest of the team resented having to stay late, but it didn't bother me: Mum wasn't getting home from work until six in the evening anyway, so I wasn't complaining about killing some time after school. Mr Johnson just assumed that I was probably more focused than the rest of the team.

Three weeks later, the All England Schoolboy Championships arrived. Our school was drawn away in the first round, which meant that we had to visit another school. Tom had managed to get me a second-hand tracksuit, a pair of boxing boots, some silk trunks and a dressing gown. I looked the part, but — more to the point — could I act the part?

We were all seen by the doctor, passed as fit to box, and were weighed-in. The judges started pairing us and I was drawn against Vic Taferelly, who had made it all the way to the All England Finals in the previous year. After leaving school, Vic went on to become a professional boxer — and that was my opponent for my first fight!

Mr Johnson and I both knew that I was going to be outmatched, and, just to prolong the agony, my fight was the last on the programme. I had to sit through all the other fights; Mr Johnson was trying to lift my morale by giving instructions as to the best way I could approach the bout. I sat and watched. I was anxious, but nowhere near as anxious as I was in those English classes.

The afternoon seemed to go on forever, and then, at last, it was time to get into the ring. Mr Johnson was acting as my second, holding the ropes open for me as I climbed in. I glanced over at my opponent who looked every inch the champion that he was. He was wearing a red silk robe with a towel on his head, his broken nose peeking out from under it. His trainer was with him, massaging his shoulders while he was shadow boxing. They really did make a fearsome pair.

I stood frozen to the spot. The bell rang a couple of times and the referee called us to the centre of the ring. He told us that he wanted a clean fight. All the time he was talking, my opponent was staring straight into my eyes. When the pep talk was over, we were told to shake hands and return to our corners.

The bell rang for the first round; he came out like a train, raining punches down on me. I managed to fight him off for a while, but then he gave me a jab that caught me off guard, hitting me square on the nose. I felt a sickening crack. It was broken. Blood poured from it.

At the end of the first round Mr Johnson managed to stem the flow of blood; however, it was difficult to breathe through my nose, which meant I had to do so through my mouth. I would have to fight with my mouth slightly open, increasing the chances of getting my jaw broken.

In the second round we stood toe-to-toe, trading punches. The blood continued to pour from my nose and, at one point, the referee stepped in between us. I thought he was going to stop the fight, which was the last thing I wanted; however, it was just the laces on my boot: they had come undone and he told me to return to my corner to have them tied. At the end of the second round my eyelids were beginning to swell, making it difficult to see. The referee came over to see if I was fit enough to continue. Mr Johnson wanted me to throw in the towel; I told him not to do that.

At the start of the third and final round, I received a jab to the mouth which dislodged my gum shield; with a couple more blows to the mouth, my teeth became embedded in my top lip, slitting it from one end to the other. A fountain of blood shot out. The referee stepped in and stopped the fight; the crowd were on their feet cheering.

With the injuries I sustained I got to stay home from school for a few days. As far as I was concerned that was no bad thing. On my return, my reputation had soared and even Mr Johnson saw me in a new light. All in all, the entire event had done me some good. I stayed with the boxing team until I left school and went on to win a few minor schoolboy championships.

I was growing-up fast, and boxing played a big part in that. A year later, with a few wins under my belt, I had moved up two weight classes and I was now boxing at lightweight. When I was fighting, it was just me and the other guy; I didn't have to rely on anyone else. When I was training or fighting, I felt a release from the anxieties I felt with life. If I did well, that was down to me; if I didn't, that was also down to me. The boxing ring can be the loneliest place in the world, and the most exciting. When I was working out or fighting, I wasn't 'the Idiot Boy' that couldn't read or write, or who had a speech problem. It was like being transported to a whole new world. It was all down to me, and when I won a fight the adrenaline rush was immense.

By now Fred had finished his National Service and was living at home with Mum and me. Being involved in illegal gambling meant that he was on the periphery of organized crime. With that and my boxing, I was gaining a little bit of street cred.

Every day tens of thousands of boys dream about making it big in sport. In South London when I was growing-up, there were two ways of making a good living: one was boxing, the other was crime. It's the same with the disadvantaged kids I work with today: they feel the only way they can make big money is either playing for Chelsea or selling drugs.

Through the school boxing team I made a small circle of friends. But I was uncomfortable with people who wanted to be with me; I would view them with a great deal of suspicion, thinking, "Why on earth do they want to be with someone like me?" Groucho Marx once said, "I wouldn't want to belong to a club that would have me as a member." My self-esteem was so low that I thought there had to be something wrong with people who wanted to be around me for any length of time.

Through boxing, I met Dave Chapman. He was also in the school team and his dad ran an amateur boxing club. Dave invited me along to the club one evening. The club gym was out of this world: it had a speed ball, a couple of punch bags, medicine balls, weights, and full-length mirrors so we could skip or shadow box in front of them; but most of all it had a boxing ring. I loved the smell of the gym, the leather and the resin. When we got into the ring a tray of resin would be placed on the floor; we would stand in it and rub the soles of our boots up-and-down — the idea was that the resin would stop us from slipping on the canvas. That smell combined with the smell of sweat — I loved it! At school there was no such luxury as a boxing ring. The gym doubled-up as the assembly hall and there were exercise bars up the walls. Mr Johnson would build a makeshift ring by putting exercise benches in a square. They were useless as we always kept tripping over them.

The first time I ever got into a boxing ring was that day when I fought Vic Taferelly, and that was one of the great advantages Vic had over me. He had ring craft; he knew how to use the ring. He would use the ropes to spring off them, pushing himself towards me with even more power; he could work me into a corner where I was trapped and was able to rain down punches on me. I think that Mr Johnson felt sorry for me: not only was I outclassed, I also didn't have access to the right equipment. It was only when our school was hosting a boxing tournament that it had a boxing ring put in; however, that was only erected on the day and was then taken down straight after the fights, allowing the hall to be ready for assembly the following morning.

Dave Chapman had an elder brother, Steve, who was also a keen boxer. Dave's dad, Sid, who enjoyed playing the role of fight promoter, daydreamed of discovering "the great British hope" among members of his club. We became friends; we went there four nights a week to train, and there were other lads at the club, which meant that I was able to widen my circle of friends.

Amateurs and pros weren't supposed to train together, but everyone did. Terry and Ronnie Lake trained there. I loved being with the pros and was picking-up little tips from them. For example, when I came out for the start of the first round, I would stamp my foot on the canvas of the ring; if my opponent jumped that would be a strong indication that he was nervous and unsure of himself. Another trick was to keep punching my opponent on his biceps, which would weaken his arms. After a while he wouldn't be able to keep his arms up, and would drop his guard; then I would move in and start landing punches on the target area, which would get the greatest number of points and the victory would be mine.

In those days boxing gloves didn't have protection on the laces; another trick was to throw a punch over your opponent's shoulder, causing the laces to graze the side of his eye. Done enough times, you could cut the eye, and the fight would be stopped.

I was once in conversation with Danny Holland, Henry Cooper's cut man. Danny told me that when Henry fought Cassius Clay in 1963 at Wembley — a year later he changed his name to Muhammad Ali — Henry let fly with his deadly right hand, known as "Henry's Hammer". It put Clay down in the dying seconds of the fourth round. The bell saved Clay from being counted out, and when he returned to his corner he didn't know what day it was. To prolong the time between rounds, Angelo Dundee, Clay's manager, cut the back of Clay's glove with his diamond ring. The fight was delayed until a replacement glove was found; that was long enough for Clay to revive himself.

In 2002, they replayed the television and radio commentaries of the fight to establish just how long the delay was. Contrary to popular belief, it was only about five seconds before the fight was restarted — not the three to five minutes that had been claimed at the time — since a spare pair of gloves had been kept at the ringside. However, what Angelo Dundee did do, which was in serious violation of the rules, was give Clay smelling salts whilst in the corner between the fourth and fifth rounds. The fight was stopped in the fifth round by referee Tommy Little because Henry had sustained a badly cut eye. He stopped the fight and awarded it to Clay, even though the scorecards had Henry ahead on points. I asked Danny if he thought that Clay had used the glove lace trick to cut the eye. He said, "Probably." Of course there is no factual basis for this assertion but it was bandied around at the time.

Arthur Holder was a local greengrocer who had managed one or two boxers in his time. He was involved in the management of Alan Minter, or "Boom" Minter as he was known to his fans. Alan won a bronze medal at the 1972 Munich Olympics; then, after turning pro, he went on to be the World Middleweight Champion. Arthur had his own gym above *The Crown* pub that was almost opposite his fruit and veg shop.

Arthur came into our club one evening. He was always on the lookout for new talent and was watching me and Ronnie Lake sparring. Ronnie was very good to the young lads in the club: he would work out with us, even though he was several weight classes above us, much fitter and had far more experience. But there was a real buzz about training with a pro, and I loved every minute of it. I always knew when I landed a good one on Ronnie because he would come back with a heavy one on my solar plexus that would almost put me on the canvas. On one occasion it did: it made me feel so sick, taking all the air out of my body. When I left school and started amateur boxing, Ronnie sometimes acted as my second.

When Sid saw Arthur in the gym, he became very suspicious; he thought he was going to take me away from the club. Following the training session, I was having a shower. Sid came into the dressing-room; he was looking very flustered. I hadn't seen him this way before: his face was as red as a baboon's backside; I thought he was going to burst a blood vessel or have a heart attack. I was sitting on a bench with a towel around me. His bald head was covered in sweat, which was running down his face. "Bob, I want you to be careful of Arthur Holder. He has poached a few boxers from this club. He promises them the world and then drops them. I reassured him that I would be careful when it came to dealing with Arthur. I was really flattered by Sid, bless him; it was the first time in my life that I felt that anyone had shown a real interest in me. If I'm entirely honest, Arthur wasn't interested in me one bit; I wasn't in his league. However, I still liked the idea of Sid trying to protect me.

In the boxing fraternity of South London there was an element of criminal behaviour — nothing too obvious. There was always a lot of wheeling and dealing going on and things happened that were not quite right. There was nothing that I could put my finger on. I'm not sure if there was any fight fixing — well, at least I don't think so — but I had noticed a couple of fights where the guys had lost on points, even though they really should have beaten their opponents. I just put it down to them having an off night — it happens to the best of us. However, they did have the same thing in common: they were all training at Arthur's gym. Thinking back, there were quite a few dubious decisions, when on paper the guys shouldn't have lost. I didn't take much notice at the time, but maybe that was what Sid was trying to protect me from. I could be doing Arthur a grave injustice, but at my level of boxing there was a lot of ducking and diving going on.

Fred told me that there was quite a lot of betting on fights. Even in amateur boxing the stakes were high; he told me that people bet on anything. He had taken a lot of bets at amateur boxing tournaments and a lot of money could change hands in one evening. He should have known: he was making a good living from illegal gambling!

At the age of fifteen I left school and there was no-one happier than me to see the back of that place. When I started there four years earlier I could just about write my name, but I couldn't spell my address, even though I had been there all of my life. When I left school four years later I was no better off — so much for so-called education. I was exactly the same as when I started. Even my modest achievements in boxing had done nothing to improve my self-confidence; my self-esteem was on the floor.

When my boxing days as a schoolboy were over, I moved up to amateur boxing and we were then governed by the Amateur Boxing Association (ABA). On the days I wasn't working, I spent a lot of time in the gym, taking my frustrations out on the punchbag or the speedball.

I started to spend a lot of time with Dave and his family. They were good to me. I would be invited to have an evening meal with them, a real treat. I started to enjoy their way of life. Sid was like a father figure to me; the family lived just a couple of streets away from my home and five mornings a week at about six am, Sid would turn up on his bike with Dave and Steve and we would set off for an hour's road work. Running around the streets early in the morning was so invigorating and Sid would shout encouragement from his bike. We did it in every kind of weather. Sid was a jobbing builder, so he would also give me one or two days' work a week, cash-in-hand.

Sid had a trophy cabinet for the boxing cups and medals that Dave and Steve had won. He kept the cabinet in a prominent place in their home; visitors couldn't fail to miss the trophies. Sid was always talking about them to anyone who would listen. I, on the other hand, didn't put my cups and medals on display. They were just hidden away because I couldn't handle success; it was such an alien concept to me. Failure was the normal mindset. I believed that I was completely undeserving, so any rewards I got must have been some sort of freak act of nature. I could see that others' achievements were well-deserved, but not mine.

With being called "the Idiot Boy" for four years, combined with the guilt trip I was having following Dad's suicide, I had hit emotional rock bottom. I felt a complete and utter failure, that I had let the school down, and the facts were staring me in the face: I could not read or write, therefore, it had to be down to me.

I started to work on building sites, the sort of employment for which I didn't need to read or write. All that I needed was brute force. When I was able to hold down a job, I was quite good. I'd turn up on time and do as much work as I could in the day. I was reliable and the site foremen would offer a better paid job as a charge hand; however, I would turn down the promotion because it meant filling in the other men's timesheets. Out of sheer panic, I would leave the job. People would say, 'Why did you do that when you were doing so well?' I would tell them that I didn't like the job, or that the foreman was always on my back. The truth was I was so ashamed; I didn't want anyone to know that I was some sort of thicko. I would spend a lot of time out-of-work, just drifting from one building site to another.

On the first Christmas Eve after leaving school, Fred and I went for a lunchtime drink. It was the first time I had been in a pub. When we walked in there were a lot of Fred's friends already inside. We went up to the bar; Fred was asked what he was drinking and he said a "light and bitter". He introduced me to the others. I was also asked what I was drinking. I didn't have a clue what sort of drinks there were; so, not wanting to look a fool, I said, "The same as Fred".

I was given a light and bitter; I started to drink it. The taste was so awful I almost choked on it — I never have liked the taste of alcohol. I was about half-way through the first pint when someone else bought another. After the second drink the taste didn't seem to matter. I had a warm feeling inside; alcohol made me feel better, and after couple of pints the world didn't seem to be such a scary place. Fred was on form with his jokes and the whole place was lively. I drank too much and had to be taken home and put to bed.

I spent the following day feeling sorry for myself and nursing a hangover. I had very little recollection of the day before. That was the drinking pattern that was set for me over the next twenty years.

On Boxing Day evening, Fred and I went out for another drink. He told me to be careful not to drink too much because some of the people he was going meet were "nasty bastards". When I met them they seemed to me to be nice people; I couldn't understand what Fred was talking about. Again, I got drunk.

Three months later, I was spending more time in pubs than in the gym. Much to Sid's annoyance, I was missing training sessions. He would try and talk to me about my drinking; he had noticed that when the four of us would go to *The Crown* for a shandy after training, I would always order an alcoholic drink, much to Sid's disapproval. Once they had finished their drinks they would head for home; I would always make some excuse as to why I had to stay. Sid would say, "I'll be round for you at six in the morning. Be ready and don't drink too much." I would claim that I was waiting to meet someone, and had no intention of drinking any more. However, I always did, and when he came round for me in the morning for training, six times out of ten I didn't get-up. I also started to let him down at work. My physical fitness began to suffer: time-and-time-again I was missing training.

Sid had been working on hosting a major tournament with a club from North London. This meant a lot to him. Dave and Steve told me that their dad had been rivals with the other club for years and so it was going to be a right needle match. It was important to Sid for our club to win. Out of respect for him I stopped drinking and threw myself into training for three weeks before the tournament.

In order to keep an eye on me during the build up, Sid had been putting a lot of work my way. When the day arrived, we spent it in the club setting up the chairs and getting the bar ready. In the afternoon we had our medicals; later, we had the weigh-ins. The local paper turned up to take pictures; we got into our kits, climbed into the ring, and all lined up with Sid in the middle. His face was a treat.

Terry and Ronnie Lake turned up to act as our seconds for the evening. About five o'clock, the other team arrived and the judges started to pair us. About six, my nerves were getting the better of me; I put my tracksuit on and slipped out for a walk. As I got near *The Crown*, I ran into Mickey Bradford. He was popping in for a drink before going over to the club to watch the fights. He asked if he could buy me a shandy.

We walked into *The Crown*. Two hours later I was drunk! Instead of contacting Sid and telling him that I was unwell and that I couldn't fight, I staggered over to the club with the intention of getting into the ring. The judges came into the dressing-room to find me drunk, where I was insisting that I was fit to fight. When I was told that I was disqualified from fighting that evening, I started to swear and even tried to take a swing at one of them, but missed. They told Sid that my behaviour would be reported to the ABA. The affair made both Sid and I look like fools; poor Sid became the laughing stock of the other team and was devastated.

That was the end of my relationship with Sid. I was thrown out of the club and he didn't give me any more work. He died ten years later. I would have attended his funeral, only I was in prison at the time.

Chapter 4

Crime doesn't pay but the hours are good

Joey Pyle

I never really embraced crime; I think it's fair to say that crime embraced me. I was engulfed by it. Now that boxing was out of my life, I didn't have any role models like Sid; and because of Fred's involvement in illegal gambling there would often be people calling at our house. These men were always well-dressed; they had nice cars and loads of money. One of them was Joey Pyle. He was among the people that Fred had warned me about that Boxing Day evening when I first met them.

On one occasion when he visited our home, he asked me if I would run an errand for him. He got out a wreath of flowers from his car and told me to deliver it to an address; he told me to tell the people that it was from him, and that I wasn't to say anything else. Then he reached into his pocket and brought out a roll of bank notes, peeled off a five pound note and gave it to me. That was a lot of money in those days and it would have taken me at least two days working with Sid to earn it; I got it for just a few minutes work. I do not know to this day what that wreath was for: was it a mark of respect for someone who had passed away, or, perhaps, did it have a more sinister explanation? All I knew was that when I delivered it there was a look of panic on the guy's face when I told him who it was from.

When I returned home, Joey was still there. He was well pleased with me because the delivery had gone okay. He said that he might have some more work for me and that he would keep in touch. He was an imposing figure: his ice blue eyes, when he stared at you, made a chill run down your spine. Yet, he was also a charismatic man. His favourite saying was, "Crime doesn't pay, but the hours are good!" I now had a new role model.

Pyle first rose to prominence in 1960 following a fight in the Pen Club, when Selwyn Cooney the club's owner was shot and died and two others were badly wounded. In the time it took the police to arrive, all but four of the club's customers had somehow suffered such catastrophic memory loss that they were unable to tell detectives where they were standing when the shooting started, let alone what they might have seen. In the weeks that followed, one of these vital witnesses was viciously attacked, his girlfriend kidnapped, beaten and slashed with a blade on two separate occasions. Another witness went missing; yet another suffered a bizarre family tragedy.

Pyle, along with Jimmy Nash and Jimmy Reed, were arrested and remanded in custody. He was up on a capital murder charge, which meant, if found guilty, he would be facing the death penalty. Three months later, the first trial would prove to be a farce: the jury were intimidated and were so terrified that the judge was forced to order a retrial. The second trial was no better: the witnesses kept changing their stories.

When it was all over, the judicial system, the police and London's underworld were all changed. The Pen Club killer—or killers—were acquitted of all but the most minor charges. Pyle and his co-defendants became some of the best known criminals in this country.

Pyle was friends with the Kray twins from their earliest days and was alongside them as they built their criminal empire. He was also able to maintain a close relationship with the Richardson brothers, who were the Krays' rivals for the criminal domination of London. Somehow, he managed to avoid the police swoops on both gangs.

At the end of the 1960s, when the Krays and the Richardsons were in prison, the age of the gangster had come to an end. However, Pyle was just getting into his stride. He played a key role in British criminal history, from the murder of Jack "The Hat" McVitie by the Kray twins, to the Great Train Robbery; from the police corruption scandals of the 1970s, to the birth of unlicensed boxing; from the biggest Payola scam in the world, to the unstoppable rise of the international drugs trade. He even allegedly had a friendship with the New York Mafia.

About ten years after the Pen Club shooting, I was having a drink in *The Crown* when Pyle walked in. He was with a couple of other guys and because of his connection with my brother Fred, I was drawn into the conversation. The subject of the Pen Club shooting came up; one man said, "Tell me, Joey, who shot Selwyn Cooney?" Pyle just smiled and said, "I haven't got a clue". The same guy asked another question: "Come on, Joey, you must know who shot him?" Pyle smiled again and said, "It wasn't me, and it wasn't Jimmy Nash or Jimmy Reed. Cooney must have walked into a passing bullet!"

When he died of motor neurone disease in 2007, there were well over a two thousand people who attended his funeral in a mile long cortege. There were show business personalities and leading figures from the criminal fraternity; however, by and large the number was made up of wannabe gangsters. A friend phoned me asking if I was going to the funeral; I told him, "What on Earth do I want to do that for? He was a friend of my brother. I'm sorry for his family, but I really didn't know him all that well; I spent more time with his brother Teddy and his cousin Terry White. I would meet him around the drinking dens of South London and sometimes we would have a chat and drink together, but I wouldn't say that he was a close friend."

The hearse was drawn by four black horses; there were so many flowers that they had to use a flat back lorry to carry them all, and hire stewards to control the crowds. The funeral got a centre page spread in the *Daily Mail*. I couldn't help wondering what the world was coming to if someone like Joey Pyle could get all of that publicity, and yet when someone else dies who has spent all of his or her life working for the benefit of others — like trying to find a cure for cancer — their epitaph would just be a few lines in an obituary column.

With nowhere to focus my energies, and still with Joey Pyle as my new role model, I was drinking more and more. However, the more that I drank, the more aggressive I became. I was getting into fights. I was also engaging in petty crime like stealing lead from roofs or scaffold clips from building sites.

By now Fred had had a couple of pulls by the police about his illegal gambling. It was also around that time that the Gaming Act came in. It was now much easier to place a bet legally and so the bottom had fallen out of Fred's market. He started to work as a window cleaner.

Finally, it had to happen: I was arrested for the first time. There were three of us and we were driving about in a stolen car; I had just turned sixteen. We were put up in front of the juvenile court and the case was put back for four weeks for sentencing so they could have the probation and school reports. Mum and Fred were putting pressure on me to join the army; if I'm honest, they thought that it would be the best way to get me out of their hair.

Within a week we had a home visit from a probation officer: that was when Mr Hamilton came into my life. Mum and Fred told him about my ambition to join the army; he said he thought it would be a wonderful opportunity for me. However, I didn't want a military career; I was just going along with them to keep them happy. A couple of days later I found myself in an army recruiting office. Feeling nervous because I would have to fill out forms, I knew that I stood no chance of getting in. The recruiting sergeant was just like Windsor Davies from "It Ain't Half Hot Mum". He passed me a load of forms and a pen and told me to fill them in. The first question was my name — no problems with that one! So far, so good. The next question was my address — and that was the end of my army career. When the sergeant saw what I had written, he gave me a ton of abuse and told me to stop taking the piss; there was no place in the army for idiots like me. He threw me out of the office, but not before I had threatened to put one on him. As I walked out I gave him a mouthful, but I also had a smile on my face. I couldn't go in the army and that was what I wanted.

Four weeks passed and it was time for our appearance before the juvenile court. The probation and school reports were ready, but there was a problem with the school report. Mr Johnson, being my form master, should have written it; I was sure that he would highlight my boxing achievements, making things look slightly better for me. However, he had been off sick for a few weeks, so it was left to the Welsh maniac to write it. I had no chance.

My co-defendants' school reports were fine, but mine was bad. The Welsh maniac had done a hatchet job on me. He said that I was disruptive in class; I think he had a point: taking all of that time out of the lessons to beat me must have been very disrupting. The poor man couldn't get on with his job! It must have been so irritating for him. He also stated that I was lazy and wouldn't carry out set pieces of work. Maybe that was because I couldn't do it, and not because I was refusing to.

The probation report wasn't much better. We were all fined ten shillings—a lot of money for sixteen-year-olds in 1960—and were banned from driving for a year. What we couldn't understand was that when the ban was over none of us would have been old enough to drive anyway! Although the other two had stolen the car and offered me a lift, I had been fully aware that the car was stolen; I got in it because I didn't want to appear chicken in front of them. So I went along.

The other two were told to sit down while the magistrates focused their attention on me. Along with the fine and driving disqualification, they placed me on two probation orders. I thought that was so unfair, all because a school teacher didn't like me. I hadn't even been the ringleader. Now I had an even bigger chip on my shoulder.

After the court hearing, Mr Hamilton took me to his office to fix our next appointment. He was a tall man; he wore a sports jacket with leather patches on the elbows, grey flannel trousers and brown polished shoes. That was the same as what other teachers wore; they were the enemy, and so was he.

Within weeks, I was drinking even more heavily than before. I would struggle to keep my appointments with the probation service; when I was there I wouldn't talk much. The poor man was really trying to engage with me, but I wasn't having any of it.

My drinking episodes were leading me to become increasingly aggressive; I was also becoming paranoid. One evening I had been drinking heavily. All the frustrations that I had been bottling up started to spill out. There were three guys in the pub that I didn't like; I had never see them before but in my drunken state I thought that they were talking about me and making jokes concerning the way I spoke. I tried to stare at them; I started goading them. They didn't take much notice of me which wound me up even more. I told the people I was drinking with that I was going to get all three of them; I was told not to be silly, just to drink up and behave myself. Just on closing time I went to the loo; when I came back I noticed that they had gone, so I made my way to the car park. They were getting into their car when I ran towards them, grabbing them and head-butting him to the floor. The other two came at me; I went to punch one of them but missed. They waded into me. I fell to the ground and they started to kick me. Due to a combination of the blows and the amount of alcohol in me, I passed out.

I didn't remember much about it; I had a vague memory of getting up and staggering home, falling through the front door and lying in the hallway. Fred was in bed, and when he heard the noise of me collapsing he came down, picked me up, and took me to bed.

The following morning my eyes were completely closed because they were so swollen and I couldn't see a thing for a couple of days. My abdomen and upper body were bruised and I had a couple of cracked ribs. I spent the best part of the following week in bed. Fred and Mum never questioned me as to what had happened. They knew I had it coming to me because of the level of my drinking; they thought that it was just a matter of time before I got a good hiding because I was becoming more and more out of order each time I drank. They were hoping that it would teach me a lesson and that it would curtail my behaviour. That week they tried to talk to me about my drinking. I was licking my wounds and so, just to keep them quiet, I agreed with them, and told them that I would do something about it. Within a week, however, I was drinking at the same levels again.

One evening I ran into Ronnie Downs in *The Crown*. I told him about how paranoid I was getting when I was drinking. He took out a small brown envelope from his pocket with five small tablets inside and gave it to me. "Here, take them, Bobby boy. They're better than any booze." I didn't ask him what they were, but quickly put them in my mouth and washed them down with my drink. It was only then that I asked him and he told me that it was "speed" (amphetamine).

Twenty minutes latter, I started to have a tickling sensation in my stomach, followed by a feeling of great energy rushing through my body. My mind was opened — this was the most wonderful drug. I was hooked from that moment on; I believed that the drug gave me new insights into life.

In a short space of time I became obsessed with drugs. I would take any drug. I was always trying to recreate that initial, incredible high, but I couldn't get that feeling of the first hit. It always fell short. I was never to hit that spot again and, no matter how much I took, it was never enough. If I wasn't near the drug I loved, I would love the drug I was near. I would take anything that was on offer.

Ronnie was dealing in speed. He would sell it in pubs, and on Friday and Saturday afternoons he would take up his place outside Tooting Broadway tube station. He would deal there while I worked for him acting as his lookout, being paid in cash and pills for my efforts.

On Friday evenings we would go to the Wimbledon Palais, one of London's top music venues in the early-1960s. Up and coming bands played there like The Rolling Stones, The Beatles, and The Who. Ronnie supplied most of them with speed and even became friendly with Keith Moon, the drummer of The Who. On Saturday nights we would go to the Cellar Club in Kingston, which would be open all night. When Sunday morning rolled around, I was in a terrible state with withdrawals; I couldn't sleep because I had taken so much speed over the weekend. Ronnie would give me sleeping tablets; I would go home, take them, and spend the next couple of days in bed.

I was a year into the probation order when one of the guys got a terrible beating from a team in Croydon and was put in hospital for a couple of weeks. The following Friday I had been drinking and popping pills for most of the day. I cannot remember much about it, but I was in *The Crown* that evening. There were a load of us there, all getting ready to go to a pub in Croydon where the people responsible for the vicious attack would drink.

I got swept along with the rest of them; before I knew it I was in the back of a Dormobile van and someone passed me a pickaxe handle. I've little recollection of the events that followed. I can't remember the drive to Croydon, but I do remember that I fell out of the van when we got there and had to be picked up by the others before following them into the pub. My memory is patchy from then on. I'm told that as soon as I walked through the door I started to smash up the jukebox with the pickaxe handle; then all Hell broke loose.

Vans full of police started arriving. I got separated from the others and was walking along the road when a police van pulled-up alongside me. They jumped out and started wading into me; I tried to fight back, but there were too many of them; they were hitting me with their truncheons in my kidneys and on the back of my legs. I almost passed out. My hands were handcuffed behind my back and I was thrown a couple times against the side of the van before being forced head first into it.

They peeled in on top of me; I was lying face down with one of them sat on my back, almost suffocating me. I passed out. The next thing I can remember is being dragged out of the van by my ankles, my face hitting the concrete ground, splitting my eye open. By the time they had finished, I was almost unrecognisable: my face had swollen up so much.

When the station sergeant saw the state of me he called for a doctor. Half-an-hour later I was being taken to the hospital to have my face stitched up; later I was returned to the police station.

The following morning was a Saturday. I was feeling like death: I had a hangover, plus I was withdrawing from speed. The CID started to interview me and from what they were saying, it had kicked off big time in *The Anchor* the previous evening. I didn't have a clue what they were talking about; I could only remember bits. They told me that two people were beaten so badly they would be in hospital for a least a week; several others, including a couple of women, also needed hospital treatment. I was going to be charged with GBH Section 20. I denied even being in *The Anchor*.

One of the CID officers was in his mid-thirties and spoke with a Glasgow accent. "Come on, Bob, we have witnesses that saw you in *The Anchor* when it started to kick off. If we were to put you in an ID parade later, I'm sure you would be picked out." I had a big problem: I had very little memory of what happened the night before. After the interview I was put into a cell. As I lay on the bed I heard the door of the next cell open and the voice of Jimmy Dance coming from inside. He was one of the others with me the night before and I called out to him. He answered, "Hang on, Bobby boy, my brief is on his way. They have also nicked Eddy." The police officers with Jimmy told him to shut up and he retaliated with load of verbal abuse.

Later that afternoon I met Noel Carpenter, the solicitor who was representing Jimmy and Eddy. He asked whether I wanted him to represent me as well. Of course I agreed. He told me that the police had no witnesses to state that I was involved in the fight, but many saying that I had smashed up the jukebox. I was going to be charged with criminal damage and they weren't prepared to give me bail until I appeared in the magistrates' court on Monday morning. He went on to say that Eddy and Jimmy were being released without charge, but he would be in court on Monday to make a bail application on my behalf. That was the start of the long relationship I had with Noel Carpenter. Later that afternoon I was charged with criminal damage and then spent the next forty hours in a police cell. If I'm honest I quite welcomed the peace and quiet: I was feeling really ill with withdrawals and my whole body ached from the head-to-toe beating I had received.

I lay on a sparse mattress on bed boards, with a thin blanket over me. I wished I could have died. Each hour seemed like a day. Every now and again they brought me in a drink and some food, but I couldn't eat anything.

Monday morning came and I was given a bowl of hot water and some soap. I managed to clean myself up a bit; my hair was matted with blood but I managed to clear some of it. I was then handcuffed to a police officer. As I stood up, I collapsed; I had to be helped into the van. In the cells below the court Noel came to see me. He told me that he had some bad news for me. He said that the police had contacted Mum and she was not willing to have me home; as a result, I was of no fixed address. He asked if there was another address that I could put forward; I told him that there wasn't. He then told me that there was little chance of getting bail.

Half-an-hour later, I had to be helped up the stairs to the court. The charge was put to me and I pleaded guilty. Bail was refused on the grounds of not having a fixed address. I was remanded in custody for two weeks while a probation report was prepared.

The police officer in the dock with me helped me down the stairs to the cells. As I was going back in, I asked where I was going to be taken and was told that it was Ashford Remand Centre, in Kent. The door slammed shut behind me. Then the reality hit: I was not yet seventeen and was on my way to prison. A deep sense of hopelessness and foreboding came over me.

My mind was numb; I just couldn't take in the events of the last couple of days. I was put in the cell. I sat there, thinking about prison, but my thoughts were interrupted by the cell door opening. Noel came in and the look on his face said it all. He told me that it was important that I got an address in the next two weeks; otherwise the chances of getting a prison sentence were high.

After Noel had gone, I just sat on the bench in the cell with my head down, staring at my hands. My mind was racing, trying to make sense of what was happening. I must have waited at least three hours for the prison van to arrive. I was escorted from the cell to the van and was then in for my second shock of the day. The van itself was large, but the inside was partitioned off into tiny cubicles less than half the size of an airplane toilet. There was no room to move. Each cubicle had a wooden bench with a small frosted glass window to let in the light. It was impossible to see out.

The door was closed behind me. I felt really claustrophobic. I could hear other prisoners talking to each other. They must have been picked up from other courts. One guard wrote my name in chalk on the cubicle door. A short while later, the van pulled out of the courtyard. I remained in there for another few hours while we went to other courts in and around South London picking-up more prisoners.

We arrived at Ashford after what seemed like a lifetime. I heard the noise of the large gates closing behind us as we moved inside the prison, and finally we came to a stop on the other side of the courtyard. A short while later, the door to my cubicle was unlocked by a burly prison officer with a clipboard in his hands. Not looking up, he called "Turney" then pointed with his pencil to the door at the end of the van.

I walked through a large gated doorway into the reception area where another officer placed me into yet another cubicle. This one, however, was much larger and there were already three other prisoners from the van in there. Very soon we struck up a conversation. They were talking about what they were in for: two of them were in for burglary and the other was there for robbery. They asked me what I was in for, and, not wanting to appear inferior with my criminal damage conviction, I lied and told them that I was also in for robbery. I then elaborated even further, saying that I had robbed a rent man, which seemed to impress them. I felt accepted into the group.

We exchanged stories until one-by-one we were taken out for our induction into the prison. When it was my turn, I was made to stand in front of a high desk similar to the one that Ebenezer Scrooge sat at in Charles Dickens' *A Christmas Carol*. Seated on a high stool behind the desk was a prison officer, peering over the top of his glasses at me. He asked my name and home address. I was then told to take off all my clothes. An inmate folded them and placed them in a box. Once naked, the reality started to dawn on me that I was in prison, locked away from the outside world. These people had absolute power and control over me. The noise of the doors and gates being banged shut and the smell of the place hit me. I felt tears welling up in my eyes; I wanted to go home. I knew I must keep a brave face at all costs because my street cred would be completely blown if I started crying in front of the people I had come in with. I fought back the tears. My thoughts were interrupted abruptly by the prison officer's raised voice: "You there, are you thick or something? Do you comprehend what I am saying to you?" I looked up; he was telling me to go into the adjoining room — the bath area.

There were six partitioned baths down each side of the room, each with only a half door; the toilets had the same half doors so that the staff could see you. From now on everything I did would be observed by staff and inmates alike. After a shallow, lukewarm bath, I was taken into another room where I was given some prison clothing and a meal. I sat with the three lads I had come in with, who seemed to know their way around the system quite well.

After we had eaten, we were each given a bedroll and then taken to the accommodation area of the prison. I was placed in a cell which had an old metal framed bed in the corner, about eighteen inches off the floor. It had a drab green bedcover made out of what seemed to be sackcloth. In the opposite corner there was a metal framed wooden table and a chair; on the table was a jug and bowl, and above it was a small mirror screwed to the wall. In the corner near the door stood a metal chamber pot that smelled of stale urine and that had obviously been well-used. That just added to the dehumanising effect of prison life.

This was the first of many prison receptions I would go through over the next eighteen years. As the door closed behind me, I was on my own; I was so traumatised that I felt sick. In less than seventy-two hours my life had taken a sinister and dramatic turn for the worse and there was very little that I could do about it. I made up my bed. I felt lonely and so out of touch with the world. Security lamps outside my cell window cast long shadows on my cell wall. I lay in bed and started to cry uncontrollably. I must have cried myself to sleep.

I was woken-up the following morning by the sound of a prison officer banging on my cell door. I got up and started to get dressed; then I heard the prison officer call-out, "Unlock" which was followed by the sound of cell doors being opened. As soon as I heard a key go into the lock of my cell door, it sprang open and I was told by the officer to "slop-out". I stood in my doorway for a moment, not knowing what to do next. I watched some inmates walk by holding their chamber pots. I picked up mine and followed them to empty it. The smell was overwhelming; it was an odour I will never forget. It was dehumanising having to go through this ritual twice a day.

I managed to get some hot water so that I could wash and shave in my cell. Half-an-hour later, we were unlocked again, this time to get our breakfast of porridge and stale bread. That morning, all twelve prisoners who came in the previous evening were taken for a haircut. Other prisoners were doing the cutting; we were herded in like sheep being sheared for a "short back and sides". Then we were taken to the prison shop where I was given a quarter of an ounce of Boar's Head, a black tobacco which resembled tar from the road surface. I was also given some writing paper and a stamp so that I could write home.

Pride would not allow me to tell anyone that I could not read or write. That night in my cell I tried to string a few words together for my mum and the following morning I put the letter into the censor's office. The next day it was returned to me because the censor could not understand what I had written or the address I had put. The only way they identified me as the writer was because a member of staff had written my name and prison number on the top of the page before they gave me the writing paper. Again, pride would not allow me to ask another inmate or member of staff to write the letter for me. I was unable to make contact with home.

I was put to work with the three other lads I had met the previous day: we had to scrub floors on our hands and knees. After a few days, I started to get into the routine of prison life. It had an uncanny feel about it. There was a sense of security about being in an institution; life outside in the world was so unpredictable, but in there I knew exactly what would happen from one day to the next. Up until that point, my life had been so chaotic and bewildering. My dad's illness and death started the chaos; my school was more like a war zone than a place of learning. My drinking had brought added chaos into my life. Prison order was in many ways safe and predictable, and the camaraderie of the other inmates was attractive. I elaborated on my fictional robbery to the other inmates; they seemed to believe me and I gained some status among them. In the prison pecking order, robbers were high up, followed by burglars and fraudsters. Then there were the alcoholics and drug addicts, and then — the lowest of the low — the sex offenders. By lying about my offence, I had placed myself high on the list. Prison life, therefore, offered me both stability and credibility.

Two weeks passed and I was returned to court for sentencing. A small part of me hoped that the magistrates would send me back to prison. Noel visited me in the cells below the court; he told me that the probation report wasn't favourable: it highlighted my drinking and my lack of employment. Well, I could hardly tell the probation officer that I was working for a drug dealer, could I?!

Noel said that he would try to get me a further probation order but that he wasn't a miracle worker. To be fair to him, he did give it his best shot, but the magistrate wasn't having any of it and I was given three months youth custody back in Ashford. On reflection, a part of me was pleased: I felt safe in prison. Out of those three months, I would serve two, plus another two weeks off for the time I had spent in prison on remand. I was released six weeks later, much healthier and fitter than when I went in. It wasn't to last. As soon as I left I was straight out drinking and pill-popping as if nothing had happened.

Chapter 5

Six months ago I couldn't spell prisoner, now I am one

Bob Turney

At the end of the 1960s I was serving an eighteen month sentence for burglary in Wandsworth Prison — or 'Wanno' as it is known by inmates. It had a reputation of being a tough prison; stories about the austere regime flew around the clubs and pubs of South London.

Although I would not admit it to anyone, somewhere deep inside of me I found something increasingly appealing about institutional living. Apart from the strange sense of security, there was no doubt that prison had introduced clear boundaries into my life that had never been there before. It was as if I had experienced a respite period from my chaotic lifestyle. However, it was beyond the prison walls that I struggled to cope with day-to-day living. There was one thing I knew for sure: prison was not a deterrent for me anymore. I had no worries about how I was going to survive. My body would recover from the relentless assault from alcohol and drugs; I had a roof over my head, food in my stomach, companionship and street cred. I was able to get hold of cannabis; I would smoke it in the evening in my cell. However, the one thing I had a problem with was the boredom. It could be mind-numbing.

Most of the time we were locked in our cells, twenty-two hours a day, seven days a week. We would get an hour of exercise in the morning and another in the afternoon. We would have to walk around the exercise yard clockwise, in pairs; we could only talk to the prisoner who was beside us; we couldn't talk to the people behind or in front. If we were caught doing that we would be placed on report, taken down to the punishment block and had to do three days "chokey"—solitary confinement. First thing in the morning we would have to take out the bed, table and chair, just leaving the bucket we used as a toilet. We had nowhere to sit or lie down; I would spend most of the day pacing up-and-down the cell for exercise. We were fed on a diet of three slices of dry bread and a mug of water, three times a day. Last thing at night, when the day staff were clocking off, they unlocked us so that we could put the furniture back in the cell.

When there wasn't a staff shortage, we were able to work in the mailbag shop, which was like a day out for us—we were allowed to have the radio on in there! We had to sow canvas bags by hand, five stitches to an inch, inevitably making our hands sore.

Despite the hostile environment of prison life, I felt safe. There was very little to do in our cells. Reading was the main pastime, and so not being able to read was quite a major drawback for me. However, the guy in the cell next to mine gave me a book and recommended that I should read it. I said that I would. It was called *The Draftsman*, and out of sheer boredom I tried to work my way through it. It was one of the most difficult things I have ever done: I trawled through it word by word, day in, day out; I could only understand about a quarter of the storyline. It was about a guy who planned and carried out bank robberies, which at least kept my interest, but my eyes would get so tired it was exhausting. I would have to keep stopping to rest every twenty minutes or so. After about five weeks I had actually managed to read a book and that was more than I had ever done. However, if I were to have been asked questions, I could only have given a limited summary of it.

The highlight of the week in Wandsworth was Thursday afternoons as we were taken to the bath house, given a bath and a clean change of underwear and a clean shirt, and then allowed to visit the prison canteen. This was merely an empty cell which had been turned into a shop, but here we would get our tobacco and matches. There was another activity that was a possible rival as the highlight of the week. On Monday evenings we had evening classes. There was art, toy making, guitar lessons — that sort of thing. It was the place to be. Here we would congregate with the prisoners from other wings; we would exchange information, place bets, pay out, and circulate drugs.

The currency in prisons in those days was tobacco. There was a lot of gambling going on and I wanted to be the bookmaker's runner on my wing. However, that meant that I would have to get on an evening class. They all had waiting lists and so it was quite difficult; the only one that was taking people was the Basic English course. Unsurprisingly, not many people wanted go on that one: those who attended were seen as a right brunch of Muppets. I was so keen to do some ducking and diving that I was willing to accept the chance of picking-up that same label. The enrolment was easy for me because when it came to filling out the application form I had the education officer do it for me — I was straight in!

For the first few weeks things went well; I was taking bets and if they won I would pay them out the following week. I was helping to circulate drugs around the prison, which meant that I was fairly popular on my wing. I would hide the cannabis in the hollow tubing of my bed frame and replace the rubber coaster on the leg of the bed. Even if they sent in the sniffer dogs, they wouldn't find it.

After about six weeks the teacher said to me, "You seem to have a problem. You don't appear to be responding to the lessons." He then asked me to write a letter to him over the coming week so that he could see what my handwriting was like. I kept stalling because I felt so ashamed of my writing; I kept telling him that I had forgotten to do it.

A couple of weeks went past and I ran out of excuses so I tried to write a couple of lines in my best handwriting. The next week I presented the letter to him. He took one glance at it and said, "I think you are dyslexic."

I remember thinking, "What's my sexual orientation got to do with the fact that I can't read or write properly?" I thought that he was calling me some sort of nonce! He told me that I could obtain help with the problem when I got out of prison. I thought that he was the one with the problem. Surely he must have known that I was "thick". My school knew that I was an educational subnormal and my family and I knew that I was stupid — what on earth was he talking about? The subject wasn't mentioned again and, a few weeks later, the classes were discontinued because of staffing problems, so there was no-one to supervise us.

It was well over fifteen years before I had the courage to address my dyslexia.

When I was released from that sentence, I got a job on a building site. I managed to keep my drinking under control for a while, but within a couple of weeks I lost my job and was once again acting as a lookout for Ronnie Downs. He was doing well; the more he sold, the more he paid me. However, I had no concept of the value of money; to me money equated to alcohol and drug vouchers. By now I was drinking more and even popping pills; Ronnie was giving them to me as someone would give Smarties to a child.

Ronnie's supplier was a little team from Mitcham. They had their own lab and were producing speed by the bucket load; and all this was done in someone's kitchen in a house behind the Mitcham Police Station! Another source of supply was from people who broke into chemist shops. Ronnie would pay next to nothing for the drugs because he wasn't quite sure what some of them were. He would dump most of the stuff, but some of it he did keep. That's where Donkey came in. We nicknamed him "Donkey" because he would laugh like one — "Heehaw, heehaw"! Ronnie would use Donkey like the Egyptian pharaohs would use slaves to test their food in order to see if it was poisoned: he would get Donkey to take the drugs to make sure they were alright.

If I was short of money and Ronnie wasn't around, I would get a packet of Liquorice Allsorts, take the liquorice out of the sweets and, with a razor, shave it until it looked brown. Then I wrapped it in silver paper and sold it as cannabis around the pubs. I sold a lot of it; I only got one comeback and then I was able to bluff my way out of it by saying that the guy who sold it to me had turned me over.

In a short time I found myself homeless as my mum wouldn't tolerate my behaviour anymore. Sometimes a friend would offer me a couch to sleep on. One cold winter evening I had nowhere to sleep, and the only place I could get some protection from the bitterly cold weather was a public toilet. I felt so alone. I tried to huddle in the corner to keep warm; I hadn't taken pills for three days and I was feeling like death. It dawned on me that the only place in this world that could offer me warmth, a bed, and put food in my stomach—plus offer me security and companion-ship—was prison. I made up my mind that I would get myself arrested—at least I would be out of the cold.

I left the toilets and made my way to some offices, which I broke into. Once inside, I telephoned the police and told them that I had seen someone breaking into the building that I was in. I put down the phone and waited for them to arrive! While I was waiting, it struck me that my reputation would be seriously damaged if I was arrested without putting up a fight or at least attempting to escape. So I had to put up some sort of resistance, but not too much.

A few minutes later the police were outside and I made my way to the back of the building. I got through a window into the yard and climbed over the wall; I deliberately kicked over a dustbin to draw the attention of the police. Once over the wall, I started to run, all the time looking over my shoulder. I could only see one police officer chasing me.

The police officer was a great deal older than I was and, to my horror, I was out-running him! So I had to slow down in the hope that he would catch up with me. Unfortunately, I was still losing him and there were no other policemen in the vicinity. I could not believe my bad luck! I slowed down even more. By now I was almost at walking pace and could hear the officer gaining on me, breathing heavily. I felt such a relief when he got close behind. He reached out and touched me on my shoulder; I fell face first on the ground, my hands behind my back, with the policeman collapsing on top of me.

He was fighting for his breath; he pulled out his whistle and was trying to blow it to summon help, but was struggling to do so — I felt like snatching it from his hand and blowing it for him. I didn't mind going to prison, but killing a police officer was a capital offence! Eventually he managed to summon help and at long last I was arrested.

I was charged with burglary and kept in a cell overnight. At least I was warm and fed. The following morning I was taken to court. I felt terrible with withdrawal symptoms; I had no medication to help, which meant I had to go cold turkey. I pleaded guilty to the charge and was remanded in custody for three weeks so the court could have a pre-sentence report prepared about me. I waited in the cell beneath the court for the prison van to pick me up and take me back to good old Wanno. The van arrived at the prison about eight in the evening; it proceeded through the infamous gates of that Victorian building, which closed behind us with a bloodcurdling bang. Only two of us got off the van and were taken into the cold and dimly lit reception area. I went through the familiar routine of bathing and putting on prison clothing. I was then taken to the cell; it was no different to any of the others that I had been in.

Apart from one hour's exercise a day, the rest of the time I spent on my own in my cell, which was good for me because I was feeling like death and couldn't be around anyone for any length of time. Within five days the withdrawals were almost complete; I was feeling much better and was starting to get orientated to my surroundings.

One afternoon, I had a visit from the prison chaplain. I despised him. The thought that anyone could believe in a God was, as far as I was concerned, beyond belief—the poor man. All he was doing was seeing if I was alright and if there was anything in his power he could do to help me. I wouldn't make eye contact with him; my whole body language reflected my disdain and I hardly said more than a couple of words to him. I felt uncomfortable in his presence.

After about a week I had a visit from another probation officer. Her name was Hilary and it was her job to write the report for the court. She was one of the most straight talking people I had ever met and she told me that there was very little chance that I would get a further probation order. In her opinion, I should get another prison sentence. I was rather pleased that she was not one of those do-gooders who came to save me and would go all out to get me another probation order. I was in prison, and that was where I wished to remain for the time being! She also went on to say that she had been to visit my mum who had told her about my drinking and drug-taking. She asked straight out if I felt that I had a problem with my drinking; of course I denied that it was a problem, minimising the whole thing by saying that I only drank occasionally. This was true to a point as most of the time I was out of my mind on drugs. I did not like her very much: her attitude had pushed a button or two inside of me.

A week later, I was back in front of the magistrates, who sentenced me to a further six months in prison. I had a visit from my mum and brother Fred in the cells beneath the court. She was almost in tears. I sat with them and promised that once I was out I would leave the drugs alone, find myself a job and settle down. She said that I could once again go and live with her if I kept out of trouble. I agreed that I would do that and, at the time, I meant it. However, like all my promises, they were empty.

Four months later, early one Friday morning, I was released from Wandsworth Prison with a few pounds in my pocket. By lunchtime I was drunk and trying to steal a car; within weeks I was back in Wanno again, serving a further six months sentence after another attempted burglary.

That was what life was like for me: in-and-out of prison. In prison, nothing much changes and there was perfect security in that. However, each time I came out of prison I noticed that most people I knew had moved on in life. They were doing different things; they had steady jobs and some were now married and had families. Prison had kept me in a state of suspended animation. I found the changing world outside prison a difficult place. All this did was to make prison life seem even more attractive to me.

I continued to drift in-and-out of prisons. Each time I was in there I would resolve that this time I would change, and each time I really meant it. My stumbling block was that I never took alcohol or drugs out of the equation. Each time I took a drink or drug I believed things would be different; each time I would be wrong. I had no choice once I took that first sip of drink or popped that first pill: the drug dictated my actions for that day.

By now I was associating with some pretty undesirable individuals, people with little or no integrity. The irony of it all was that they felt that I was the undesirable one and would try and distance themselves from me; to them I was alright in small doses.

By the time I was released from yet other prison sentence in April 1971, my old mate Mickey Bradford was married with a couple of small kids. He had his own small building firm, which consisted of his brother and a couple of other people. He would give me the odd day's work, in addition to which I would also make some extra money from the odd bit of skulduggery. Ronnie had upped his operations and was now selling cocaine. The speed lab behind Mitcham nick had been closed down; he was now operating in the West End, working the clubs, mixing with show business personalities, and making loads of money in the process. He took me with him on nights out. I was rubbing shoulders with famous people; I went to parties in Mayfair. Ronnie had so much money he would pay me to act as his minder, which was ridiculous: I was so out of it I couldn't even look after myself. About ten years later, Ronnie went off the radar. There were a lot of rumours floating about that he been murdered by rival drug dealers, and that his body had been doubled-up in a coffin with someone's little old grand-mother and been buried with her—quite a common way to dispose of unwanted bodies I am told. But I'm not sure; I think he knew that his luck might have been running-out and slipped out of country, or is still living here under a new identity. For all I know he might be back in South London.

In *The Crown* where I drank, there were always fights; it got so bad that the landlord had to employ bouncers to keep a lid on it. We got the right hump with that idea: we thought that he could have paid us to mind the place for him. However, it was us causing the trouble in the first place! One evening there were a few of us drinking there. We were getting the hump more and more with the bouncers so some of the lads came up with the idea that we would teach them a lesson. Chris Smith had just turned pro as a heavyweight; he was a big lad — his neck was almost as thick as my thigh — he was six feet four and had a shaven head. I would watch him train in the gym above the pub. He would get me to hold the punchbag and put all my weight behind it; he would hit it so hard that I would take off, clinging to the bag.

On that evening, I was well out of it. I told Chris that I would happily pick a fight with one of the bouncers; he said that he would be right behind me. I thought that if I were to go out, I would go out in style. One of the bouncers was leaning on the bar; he was as big as Chris, and there I was, five feet nine and eleven stone when soaking wet. This particular guy wore a "syrup" — rhyming slang for wig (syrup of fig). I walked up to the bar and asked the barmaid if she could fetch me a salt cellar from the kitchen. Without asking questions she turned and walked towards the kitchen; the bouncer exchanged a half grin. Then the barmaid returned and handed me a salt cellar; I sprinkled some salt on the bouncer's shoulders and said, "There you go, mate. That will make the syrup look more realistic. Now it looks like you have dandruff on your shoulder!"

The guy went ballistic and made a grab for me; in a split second, I saw my whole life flash before my eyes. Just as he was going to hit me, Chris stepped in with a devastating right hook, sending the guy's head rolling back, dislodging the syrup and causing his eyes to roll as the bouncer dropped to the floor, bald as a badger. He was out cold. All hell broke loose; it was like a scene out of a John Wayne film with tables, chairs, bottles and glasses smashing everywhere. I grabbed a leg from a broken bar stool and ended up by the door. I stood there hitting anyone who was trying get out.

The pub had to be shut for three days whilst the mess was cleared up. The police turned up but they were met with a wall of silence: the place was packed that night but no-one could remember what had happened.

That was the end of the bouncers. When the pub re-opened three days later, the landlord employed Chris and a couple of others to look after the place. There was no more trouble.

Scamps was a local nightclub. I got wind that they were paying their bouncers ten pounds a night and all that they could drink. To an alcoholic that was heaven: getting paid to drink! I kept pestering the manger for a job, but he was not having any of it as my reputation as a drinker and pill popper had preceded me. As far as he was concerned I was too unpredictable. The fight at *The Crown* was a talking point for weeks; there was a lot of speculation flying about and my name was linked with it as one of the main players. I did nothing to dispel the rumours.

I was in Scamps having a drink and chatting to one of the doormen about the fight, grossly exaggerating my involvement of course. He told me to wait there as he went into the manager's office. A couple of minutes later he reappeared with the manager; both came over to me and ordered me another drink. The manager said, "Kenny told me that you can handle yourself. We had a couple of people jack it in last night. The job is yours if you want it. Be here at eight o'clock tomorrow night with a black tie and suit. It's a tenner a night plus drinks."

The following evening I was there, suited and booted, ready to start. The manager took me into the office and gave a pep talk about pacing myself when it came to my drinking; he told me that the staff often stayed behind after the club closed in order to have a good drink. With that I left the office, went straight to the bar and ordered a large scotch and lemonade with ice. After I had thrown that one down my throat, I had a walk round the club; there was no-one in yet, so I went and had a couple more drinks and, feeling bored, popped into the back office to take some pills. About half-past-nine the place started to fill up. I don't remember much after that.

The following morning I woke up in bed at Mum's place. The suit was thrown across the floor; I had blood caked around my nose; my left eye was slightly swollen. I picked up my shirt to find that most of the buttons were ripped off and that there was blood down the front of it. I thought that there must have been a fight in the club and that I got injured stopping it.

That evening I turned up at the club only to be met at the door by the manager who had a cut on his nose and two black eyes. With him were two bouncers. As I tried to walk in the door, I asked him what happened. He said, "Out of here. You're sacked!" I asked why; he told me that he paid me to stop fights, not to start them. Apparently, the night before I had started a fight with a customer at the door; the manger came to see what I was doing and I head-butted him. I had absolutely no memory of that.

A couple of days later, Mickey offered me some work which I was pleased to take up. On the way to work in the morning, Mickey and his brother would talk about their marriages and their kids—I really envied them. I desperately wanted some sort of stability in my life. I was now twenty-seven-years-old and had noticed that most of the people my age were married, had small children, and seemed to be happy. I was far from happy.

I decided that what I needed in my life was a good woman who would sort me out. I needed to get married. However, in the past my love life had not been too successful. Even if I took someone out on a date, I would take them to a pub and spend the evening drinking and trading insults with other people. Sometimes that would also include my date and that would be the end of that relationship. If I did have a longer relationship with anyone it would end in me abusing them verbally to the point where they couldn't stand it any longer. My self-esteem was so low; I had a real loathing for anyone who wanted to be around me. I felt that there must be something wrong with them if they wanted to have anything to do with me. So where on earth was I going to find someone who would want to marry someone like me? I had never been able to form relationships and would just take hostages. I was so insecure within myself that I would want to be around that person twenty-four hours a day and could not bear to let them out of my sight. I was so paranoid that, if they were away from me for any length of time, they would desert or dump me for someone else.

One evening, I was drinking in my local pub and I ran into a young woman by the name of Pam. She had dated a friend of mine and had been present when we had done some shady deals with stolen property. I asked her how she and my friend were getting on; she told me that he had dumped her for someone else. She poured her heart out to me about how depressed she was about her relationship ending. We spent the rest of the evening talking and drinking. She told me that she found relationships with men difficult and that she always wanted more than other people were prepared to give her. She was only nineteen and very vulnerable. I had found my next hostage.

Chapter 6

**Probably the only place where a man can feel really secure
is in prison, except for the imminent threat of release**

Germaine Greer

W ithin a few days, Pam wanted to be with me 24/7. She believed we had a lot in common: she also came from a large dysfunctional family. Her father had only recently remarried after her mother had committed suicide by gassing herself. On reflection, from the start of our relationship she was showing signs of co-dependence. Co-dependents tend to get involved in toxic relationships with people who are unreliable, emotionally unavailable and needy. Well, I certainly ticked all of those boxes!

Pam was so insecure that she defined herself as a victim; as a result she would always forgive my outrageous and insulting behaviour when I was drunk for fear that I would leave her. I took that as an open licence to behave in any way I wished. Within days of meeting, she was telling me that she loved me. As for me, after years of substance abuse, I was emotionally disengaged; I wasn't sure how I felt about anything. I was almost dead inside.

Within a few weeks we had moved in together, if that is what you could call it. Physically, I wasn't there most of the time; emotionally, I wasn't there at all. I would disappear for days on end, usually stuck in some squat, completely out-of-my-head on drugs. It was in these places that I was introduced to opium and acid (LSD).

Pam was my "enabler": each time I returned home, she would feed me, run a bath, and let me sleep off the effects of the drugs. She would always justify my behaviour, all the time enabling me to carry on with what I was doing.

There was a local villain by the name of Eddy who fancied himself as a bit of a hard man. He was always threatening to shoot people. Once, I had made a comment about his wife; I said, "She looks like a bulldog chewing a wasp." Eddy soon got to hear about that one.

One evening, I was having a drink and a chat with an old mate of mine, Terry, in *The Crown*. Suddenly there was a loud bang and the swing doors flew open to reveal Eddy standing there in the doorway, looking like Clint Eastwood. All that was missing was the theme music from *The Good, the Bad and the Ugly* playing on the jukebox. Eddy walked towards me, his eyes bulging like organ stops. He looked a very angry man. Half way across the room he was screaming that he was going to kill me. From under his overcoat he produced a sawn-off shotgun. I started to laugh at him, which only aggravated him more; people in the pub were diving for cover and the landlord ran into the back office to phone the police. I laughed even more when I noticed Terry creeping-up behind him with a great big ice bucket, which he promptly put over Eddy's head, pushing him to the floor. He was lying there with the bucket on his head; I picked up the gun and pointed it at him. The landlord shouted, "Leave it out, Bob; the Old Bill are on their way." I dropped the gun. Terry and I made a run for the other door just as the police started to arrive. Eddy was arrested and got two years; Terry and I got clean away.

In the early-1970s colour televisions were coming online and Terry and I would steal them to order; we would either get them from houses or ram-raid shops. Television rental shops like Rediffusion, DER and Radio Rentals, all had ceiling to floor windows; we would just reverse a van through the window and get as many sets as we could. The best time to do it was in the early hours of Monday or Tuesday morning; we worked out that most people had early nights on a Sunday and Monday, and so hardly anyone would be awake. We would smash through the window between one and two am. If people were woken-up by the sound of a window going in they normally waited to hear if the noise happened again before they got out of bed to investigate; if there wasn't a second crash, they normally turned over and went back to sleep. Most of the time it worked, and as we drove away there were always very few bedroom lights coming on.

It was a nice little earner: we would get £100 each for the TVs and were never short of buyers — in fact we had a waiting list! People would be more than happy to pay more if it meant they could jump the queue. We even provided an after sales service: we had a television engineer who would go round and repair any sets that became faulty. He wouldn't ask any questions; he was only too pleased to get the extra money. In fact, we would sometimes strike deals with him where we would pay him for information as to where we could get sets from — he was making a lot of money! And so were we, Terry and I, earning a grand a week between us, which was a lot of money back in the early-1970s. However, we never had any of it left; we just kept partying all the time. I wasn't even paying the rent, so Pam and I would have to move around a lot.

We had been together for seven months when she told me she was pregnant. She always wanted to be married and have a family; she was in love with the idea of being married and to her way of thinking she really didn't care who it was with. She had a couple of elder sisters who were already married with families — all she wanted was to be like them.

I, on the other hand, didn't want to get married, but I agreed anyway just to shut her up. My family was pleased because they felt that this woman would have a positive influence on me and that I would start behaving in a responsible way. However, the thought of becoming a father did have some impact on me. I told Terry that I thought now was a good time to call it a day; our activities with the stolen TV sets were getting a lot of publicity and the police were under pressure to get a result. We were featured on the crime television programme "Police 5" and every week there was a two-page spread in *The Sun* about us.

Lots of shops were beginning to install security grills on their windows, and, on top of all this, our customers had started to dry up. Luckily, I managed to get my old job back with my mate, Mickey. He paid me cash-in-hand, which was very useful. I seemed to steady myself a bit: I was holding down the job and my drinking and drug-taking were confined to the weekends.

June 1972 saw the birth of our son David. I was present at the birth and it was one of the most moving things I have ever witnessed. Another three months went by and we were offered a brand new council maisonette, as the three of us were up until then living in just one room. It started to slowly dawn on me that I had responsibilities in life now; but I wasn't able to look after myself, let alone a family. We settled into our new home and I managed to hold it together until after Christmas. Inasmuch as I could feel any healthy emotion, I did enjoy being a father. David was a wonderful baby and I would try to spend as much time with him as I could. I yearned to be like the other fathers I knew, but the emotional pain I was in because of my past prevented me from fully bonding with him.

By the beginning of 1973 I found myself out-of-work. The moment I woke up in the morning, I was either drinking or smoking cannabis. I would make my way to the pub to meet Terry and would remain there drinking until the afternoon, when we would go out to burgle some houses and sell our ill-gotten gains. It was then back to the pub for another bout of drinking and drugs. I would get home in the early hours and fall into bed; in the morning I would get-up and start all over again. Sometimes I would not leave home for days on end and would just sit around, drinking myself into oblivion. There were times when I would fall asleep in the armchair and not go to bed for days — a chilling reincarnation of my father and his illness. Then there were the times that I would not get out of bed at all and send Pam out to buy my alcohol. If I was in a bad mood she would keep herself and the baby out of my way by going to visit her family.

Occasionally, Terry would call round and entice me out of my room; I would have a bath, get dressed and tell Pam that I was just popping-out to the pub for a couple of hours. I would then disappear for days, without calling home to say that I was alright. I would return without any explanation as to where I had been. Pam was always there to clean me up and cook me a meal before I went to bed. I'm sure that in her mind she felt she was doing the right thing.

One evening I was arrested for driving a stolen car. I was hoping that I would be sent to prison; it was the only place where I could find refuge from the responsibilities of life and the continuous emotional pounding I seemed to be going through. However, the court took a lenient view because I was now a married man with a family and so put me on probation one last time — my final chance to put my life in order. My marriage had started to disintegrate; I had mounting debts as I spent nearly everything I had on alcohol and drugs; the rent wasn't being paid and we were at risk of being evicted. On top of that, Pam was pregnant again.

Hilary was still my probation officer and, like before, was very direct with me. She would ask me questions, like, "Have you ever stolen money to buy drink and drugs?" Of course I denied that I had: by admitting it I would only be conceding that I was an alcoholic and drug addict. She would not stand any of my nonsense and told me that, in her opinion, I was an alcoholic. I was outraged; so much so that I went out and got drunk! Hilary was valuable to me in that she was the only person who continually challenged my lifestyle. She was the only stable influence in my chaotic existence and she worked hard to get me to recognise my substance abuse. She was the only person who was willing to say that I had a serious addiction.

At this time, I was so desperate for money I didn't know which way to turn. Terry called round with a friend, Gordon. They took me out for a drink and told me that they had a bit of business they wanted to talk about. Gordon's ex-girlfriend had worked in a large electronics factory that employed hundreds of people; he had found out that the wages bill was enormous, at least ten grand a week. The money was collected from a local bank in a saloon car by just two people on a Thursday afternoon. He asked if I was up for having some of it; my answer was, "Does the Pope have a balcony! Of course I'm up for it."

The next day was a Thursday. It was agreed that we would meet in *The Crown* that lunchtime and go and suss out the wages run. At three o'clock the car drew up; one guy got out and went into the bank. Five minutes later he re-appeared carrying a bag, got into the car and drove-off. We followed him back to the factory.

We decided that the best place to tackle him was on the pavement outside the bank. It was agreed that Terry and Gordon would do the snatch and drive; if needed I would take care of the driver of the saloon. It was also down to me to sort out the wheels. I had a large key ring full of worn ignition keys that I had got from a mate who worked in a car breakers yard. Over the weekend I managed to get an S-Type Jaguar; I just put one of the keys in the lock and—hey presto—we had our getaway vehicle! It was so easy. I parked it in the garages beneath our maisonette.

Most of that week was spent at home. I wasn't drinking that much—well, only "a couple a day" just to stop the shakes. On the Wednesday evening I went out and stole a mini-van and parked it about a mile from the bank on a housing estate. The follow day, Terry and Gordon came round to my place. Gordon had a holdall with him; in it were three boiler suits, gloves and balaclavas. We were all roughly the same build and so, if dressed the same, it would be difficult for any potential witnesses to make a positive identification. He also had a hand gun. "What's that for?" I asked. "Oh, that. That's in case anyone gets leery. I'll stick it in their boat race (face). Don't worry; it's not loaded."

We went to the garage, hopped into the S-Type, and parked where we could see the bank. We put on the boiler suits and sat there for what seemed like an hour — it was no more than ten minutes. We saw the car with the two men from the factory in it. Entering the roundabout, we started to follow it. It drew-up outside the bank and I pulled-up just behind it. One of the men got out and walked into the bank; it seemed like an eternity before he reappeared with the bag of money.

We pulled down our balaclavas. In an instant Terry and Gordon were out of the car and on the pavement. Terry grabbed the bag of money; Gordon pushed the guy to the ground. As the driver of the car was about to get out to help, I drove up close beside him so that he couldn't. By now Terry and Gordon had run round to the right-hand side of the Jag and had got into the back seat. With wheels spinning, we sped away. I looked in the mirror; the guy who had had the money was now getting back into the car and they started to chase us. They soon gave up when Gordon waved the gun at them.

We all started to scream when Terry looked into the bag and said, "There must be at least ten grand in here!" Within five minutes we were in the housing estate; we got out of the Jag and ran through an alleyway to where the mini-van was parked. This time I drove-off slowly. As we were heading to Gordon's place, there were police racing at high speed towards the bank.

Once at Gordon's we counted the money. There was just over twelve grand. That was a huge amount of money in those days, especially if you consider that a decent three bedroom house would cost less than that. I jumped on a bus to go home with just over four grand in a brown paper bag. The bus had to go past the bank; there where police everywhere. There was also a police helicopter trying to find the Jag. The bus slowed down as it went past. The other passengers were looking out of the windows; a couple of old dears were saying that there had been a bank robbery; then someone else chipped in to say that they believed someone had been shot. I sat on that bus with a grin on my face.

I got home and emptied the contents of the bag onto the kitchen table. Pam and I had never seen such an amount of money before. We just sat there and stared at it.

During the next few days Pam was running everywhere paying all the outstanding bills. The phone had been cut off and the council was almost at the point of evicting us, so the rent arrears were paid and the phone was put back on. She ordered a washing machine, new furniture and got people in to decorate the place. We all had new clothes and I could drink and have as many pills as I wanted.

After about three days, Terry and Gordon paid me a visit; they were worried about the level of police activity and it was felt that we should go somewhere out of the way for a little while. I suggested we went to Jersey; the only reason I said that was because there was very little tax on alcohol there and so I could get even more booze for my money. So off I went, leaving Pam with some money, a three-year-old child, and almost eight months pregnant.

The three of us headed for Gatwick Airport. By the time we got there we had already had a few drinks. Somehow we managed to board the plane and soon we landed in Jersey. We asked a taxi driver to take us to a good hotel; he took us to a four star one overlooking the sea. We tried to book in but were told that the place was full; however, if we were prepared to share a room for the next three days then after that we would be able to have our own rooms. We didn't mind that — it was better than going all over the island trying to find something else.

We made our way to the room, got changed, and then headed straight down to the bar for a drink. We weren't in there for more than ten minutes before we discovered why the hotel was full and we why we were sharing a room: there was a three-day police convention being held. The place was full of the Old Bill!

Instead of booking out and going to find another hotel, we remained in our room for three days, drinking and having meals sent up. We stayed in that hotel for a month before Terry got into a fight with one of the guests and so we had to head back to London very quickly.

I had been back for just over a week when our second son Paul was born. Again I was present at the birth and my heart overflowed with joy. I had tears in my eyes as I held my newborn son, but there was also a great feeling of despair as I knew deep inside of me that I could not cope with the responsibility of my growing family.

Within a short space of time, the money had run out; I was once again unemployed and started drinking and taking drugs on a daily basis. Things were also really bad with Pam: she had found out that I was having an affair with one of her friends. I wasn't living at home; I was roughing it, sleeping on friends' sofas. Terry's partner had walked out on him so I moved into his flat.

By now I had returned to crime and was arrested again. I was caught bang to rights breaking into a house. I was completely off my head on alcohol and pills and a neighbour had seen me breaking in. I had very little recollection of doing it; all I remember was that I was having drinks with Terry and trying to convince him to come with me. However, because of the problems he was having in his relationship, he wasn't interested; he just wanted to drown his sorrows.

I must have tried to do it on my own. I didn't have a car with me and, if I am to be completely honest, I wanted to get done. With the way I was feeling I really didn't mind going back to prison. The thought was quite appealing: at least I would be able to cope in there a lot better than I could on the outside.

I was remanded in custody and taken to Brixton Prison. The police objected to bail because I had no fixed address; when they went round to my place to search it, Pam had told them that I no longer lived there and that I wasn't likely to return.

When I arrived at Brixton it was late in the evening. I was going through terrible withdrawals. I was in a right state: shaking, sweating, and I had body cramps. As it was so late the doctor had gone; all I was offered was a couple of paracetamol, which did nothing to help. I lay in my cell that night hallucinating; I was seeing things creeping-up the wall; I was having cold sweats. The other guy in my cell thought that I was raving mad. I didn't sleep a wink; it was one of the longest nights of my life.

The following morning, I was lining up with at least ten others to see the doctor. Due to my abuse of amphetamines, I had become grossly underweight; my hair was like straw, my eyes were bloodshot, and some of my teeth were falling out. The doctor gave me some lithium in liquid form for the withdrawals — we used to call it liquid handcuffs because we would be like zombies for days until the withdrawals subsided.

In the queue I could barely stand; I was propping myself up against the wall when a Salvation Army officer walked past the line. She turned around and walked back to me. She looked me in the eyes and said, "How old are you?" I replied, "Thirty-two". Then she said, "You know what they say about men of your age who are still going into these places?" Not waiting for an answer, she continued: "That you'll be coming in-and-out of prisons for the rest of your life!"

Well, that remark certainly didn't go unnoticed. It had pushed a button inside of me and after all the years I had been in denial about myself, she managed to penetrate my defences; to dislodge a few bricks in the walls I had built up around myself since I was a child. When she said that, I wanted to hit her, but I was too weak to even offer a reply. I just stood there and took it. In my mind I dismissed her as some sort of crackpot, one of those nutty do-gooders. I started to retreat behind that wall of denial I had built but it was never going to be the same again: someone had breached my defences. For some time I wondered why she chose me to pick on; but harking back it's quite clear that I must have looked such a pathetic and pitiful sight compared to the rest of the men I was with.

I was in Brixton for six weeks. I would be taken to court each week; my solicitor Noel Carpenter said my best chance of bail would be at the committal hearing if I put forward a suitable address. My brother Fred offered to put me up at his place — the police couldn't object to that. I was granted bail with the condition that I would have to sign in at the local police station between six and seven pm each day. I was committed to Kingston Crown Court for trial.

I hardly stayed at Fred's place; most of the time I would live in squats. I would go round to Pam's and she would let me see the kids, but she had no intention of us getting back together.

By now Terry had gone AWOL. No-one seemed to know where he had gone. I had asked around his family but they didn't have a clue. Gordon was on remand for another robbery for which he later received ten years.

In November of that year I was up at Kingston Crown Court. I changed my plea to guilty and was sentenced to two years. That night I went through what was, by now, the very familiar routine of the Wanno reception. I had very little contact with the outside world apart from visits from Fred, who would bring David with him. On one visit David told me that mummy had a man called Mick living with her. I was devastated; I had been hanging-on to the hope that, once I was out, Pam and I would be reconciled. I managed to write a few lines to Pam asking her if it was true about her having a new partner and she wrote back confirming that it was. I sank into feeling extremely low; my moods would range between depression and hatred for Pam. Suicide was at times uppermost in my mind. The more depressed I became, the more I would withdraw into myself. The only relief I got was to smoke cannabis, which I would occasionally get from friends I knew on the outside. I would get letters from Hilary who would visit me every now and then. She was working on getting some accommodation for me for when my release came.

I was let out in January, 1978. I managed to get a job with my old mate Mickey. I visited Pam and the kids and was filled with resentment because they all seemed to be enjoying a happy family life. Pam's new partner had taken over from me — mind you, I wasn't a hard act to follow as a father! There was really not much of a role for me to play in my sons' lives. David did know me but Paul was unsure and was now calling his stepfather "Daddy". Pam was only tolerating my visits to see the children because she felt that if she stopped I would start trouble.

There was an unspoken law that no-one messed about with someone's wife or girlfriend when they were inside. I was expected to do something about this guy who had muscled in on my family while I was in prison. I was always being asked by the local hard nuts whether I had broken Mick's legs yet; they knew some people who would be only too willing to do it for me. I said I was working on it. I had to save face with the people I was associating with and I could not let them think that I had gone soft on them.

After a night's drinking, I felt I had to do something. I could not face being thought of as a failure by these people. We went and got some iron bars and hammers, jumped into a car and made our way over to Pam's house. I banged on the front door and screamed. Pam appeared at the bedroom window as I started to smash the front door down. By now the neighbours were out and the police were on their way. I was pulled back by a friend who told me to run for it. Before I left, I noticed that Mick's motorbike was outside the house. I tried to set fire to it, then got into a waiting car and drove-off at top speed.

The police were looking for me and I had nowhere to go. The only person I could think of was this nutter from Yorkshire called "Dog End" because his name was Arthur Fagg. I spent a couple of days with him; we drank cider and smoked Woodbines. He was a shoplifter and when we had drunk a couple of bottles of cider each, he would take me along with him. He was a master at it: we would go into one shop and he would steal a suitcase; then we would go into another and he would fill the suitcase up. I would watch in amazement.

One day Dog End was pulling the old suitcase routine when an off-duty police officer saw us and we were arrested. I ended up getting another year for endangering life by trying to set fire to the motorbike.

I was released again from Wanno in May 1979. I came out of there with no hope. I didn't know what was going to happen. I kept hearing the voice of that Salvation Army officer who had spoken to me in Brixton Prison; she was right that all I had ahead of me was a life in prison. I had nowhere to go; I felt so lost and lonely and at the time was sleeping rough. I would beg from the people passing by. If someone put a few coins in my hand it would slightly warm my frozen heart: they had recognised me as a human being. When I approached people to ask for money, most of them would just look the other way. To them I was invisible; I didn't exist; I was nothing. There were those who would spit at me.

In between living on the streets, I would stay in squats. In early June 1981, I woke up in a dirty room on a filthy mattress. I was soaked in my own stale urine and covered in vomit. As I lay there trying to make some sort of sense of what was going on, I heard a scratching noise by my right ear: it was a rat trying to burrow into the mattress. I just lay there. Tears were rolling down my face; I wanted to die. Death would have been a happy release for me and so I decided to end my life.

After what seemed like hours — I'm sure it wasn't that long — I managed to get-up. I struggled to walk; I was unsteady on my feet. I had enough money on me to buy a quarter of a bottle of scotch — I needed that to steady my shaking hands because if I didn't have steady hands I wouldn't be able to cut my wrists with the rusty penknife that I had. I managed to walk the few hundred yards from the squat to the off-licence. As I walked in, the look on the face of the woman who served me was one of total shock; I gave her a handful of change and she passed the bottle. I couldn't make it back to the squat. There was a public toilet across the road and I managed to make my way into one of the cubicles. I downed the scotch in one; it was burning my throat as it went down. I took a deep breath. The shakes subsided enough so that I could open the penknife and then plunge the blade into my wrist. After a few moments, I passed out.

Chapter 7

It's not the mountain we conquer, but ourselves

Sir Edmund Hillary

I came round. I was lying on the wet floor of the toilet cubicle; the door was open and I could hear someone talking: "There's an old tramp in there. He's tried to top himself. He's in a right mess and he stinks of piss. Don't go in there; my mate has called an ambulance. If you want my opinion, he is better off dead, the state he's in."

I tried to get-up but I fell again. One of the voices said, "Don't move, mate; help is on its way." I tried to get-up again; this time I managed to sit on the toilet. I had blood pumping out of my wrist; I was bent over; I started to wet myself again, and by now there were two men standing at the door looking at me. "Look at that dirty old tramp. He is pissing himself again!"

Just then two ambulance men appeared; one of them said, "Come on, old son, let's have a look at your wrist". I tried to push him away, but I was too weak. I just wanted to be left alone. I wanted to die. The first one put a bandage on my wrist; the other a blanket around my shoulders. "We're just going to pop you along to the hospital," one of them said.

At the hospital I had twelve stitches put in the wound in my wrist. They took off all my clothes and the nurse gave me a bath, washed my hair and beard, which were matted with vomit, then helped me into a hospital gown and dressing gown. The sister came in and said that she had phoned my brother Fred and he was going to bring in some fresh clothes. After that, I would be able to go home.

When I saw Fred I started to cry uncontrollably. "Come on, mate; it's not bad," he said. "Here, put some of my clothes on." He then turned to the nurse: "I'll take him home with me." When I was dressed, another nurse came in and said, "I've made you an appointment for Dr Gayford's clinic in Thornton Heath for tomorrow afternoon at two. He is a good man; he does excellent work with people like you." I said, "What do you mean 'people like me'?" "Alcoholics" was the reply. I was too drained emotionally to come back at her; I wanted to say, "What do you mean 'alcoholic'?!"

Fred took me back to his place. His wife Carol cooked me a big fry up but I couldn't eat a thing. Then she cut my hair and gave me a shave. Fred was supplying me with a limited amount of scotch to stop me from going into withdrawals — I took hold of the glass with both hands because I was shaking so much. He sat beside me and put his arm around my shoulders. That act of compassion was such a gentle moment between us.

The following lunchtime a friend of the family offered to take me to the clinic. We arrived dead on two and I was seen by one of the nursing staff for an assessment of my drinking. I really didn't believe at that time that I was a full-blown alcoholic; I considered myself borderline. After all that I had been through in the last twenty years, I was still deceiving myself. "I wasn't *that* bad. Maybe I was a *little bit* alcoholic", I thought. That is about as ridiculous as a woman thinking that she was a little bit pregnant — she's either pregnant or she isn't. Being an alcoholic is as black and white as that; there are no half measures. But many of us will deceive ourselves for years, believing that we can control it, sometimes with fatal results.

After I had been seen by the nurse, I was told to sit in the waiting room and that the doctor would see me soon. I waited for a little while feeling terrible and all I wanted to do when I was shown into the doctor's office was to leave. He was an elegant looking man with greying hair and piercing blue eyes. He introduced himself and invited me to sit down. He sat there, reading the notes his staff had made about me, then said:

"Do you want to stop drinking?"

"Yes I do," I replied.

He went on:

"The programme I run is tough; compared to me, the Ayatollah is a liberal!"

He told that me that he ran the Minnesota Model: basically the first five steps of the twelve step Alcoholics Anonymous (AA) programme. He went on to say that he would admit me into the unit, but the condition of residence would be that I would have to attend five AA meetings a week. He told me that he was admitting me straightaway; that I should go to the hospital and once there find my way to Pinel House where the staff would be expecting me.

I was driven to the hospital feeling that my life was over. I could not live with alcohol and I could not live without it. I wondered what was going to become of me. As we drove through the grounds of the hospital, the withdrawals seemed to intensify. We followed the signs to Pinel House, which was set back from the main hospital. It was a single story building with a long driveway up to the front door. As we pulled-up, a nurse was coming out of the main entrance; she walked up to my door, which the driver had already opened, and helped me out. She held me by the arm; I was so unsteady on my feet. She said, "You must be Bob. We have been expecting you. Do you need a wheelchair?" I thought to myself, "Leave it out, love; I'm not that bad. I'm thirty-six, not ninety-six." I told her that I would be fine without one.

Once inside the unit she took me to my room, which was next door to the staff office. There was an internal widow in the room from which I could see into the office. The nurse noticed the puzzled look on my face. She explained that I would be in this room for a short time because they were concerned that I might be a suicide risk. She reassured me that it would be only for a few days and then I would be able to move in with the rest of the patients. She told me that she was going to get me something to help me with my withdrawals. Soon she was back with a couple of Heminevrin tablets, which would take the edge off my discomfort. She watched me take the medication and then I was shown to the television lounge.

There were two patients who had also been admitted that afternoon. They introduced themselves as Jill and Tony; they offered me a cigarette and we started a conversation. Jill was in her mid-thirties and had been admitted for detox on a number of occasions before. She took great relish in telling me all about the unit. She had been drinking for a number of years, but she really had to stop this time because her husband had had enough and was threatening divorce if she did not do something about it.

By now the Heminevrin had started to kick-in, and I was feeling much more comfortable and rather light-headed. Tony was a school teacher who was also in his mid-thirties. He spent the best part of half-an-hour telling Jill and myself that he could not understand what he was doing in a place like this. He only came in to keep his family and his employers off his back. According to Tony they had it all wrong—sure he admitted he liked a drink, but no way was he an alcoholic. He said that he would be going home in a few days when everyone realised what a mistake they had made putting him in there.

When Tony had finished trying to justify his drinking to us, we were joined by other patients who had come out of a group therapy session. These people had already been in for a week or two.

Five minutes later another member of staff told us that our evening meal was ready. Jill showed me into the kitchen where we collected our food and then took me into the dining-room. She explained that we could sit at any table, but the one by the window was reserved for "the Group". She explained that the Group was made up of patients that were going through Dr Gayford's intense therapy programme and were accommodated in a separate part of the building away from us mere mortals. Jill spoke of them with reverence as if they were some kind of elite body. It was Jill's ambition to be selected for that group. As we were talking, a group of people came in wearing identical tracksuits and took their places at the table by the widow. Poking me in the ribs with her elbow, Jill told me in a low voice that they were members of the Group. They did not look any different to the rest of us apart from wearing those same tracksuits. Maybe Jill knew something I didn't.

After our evening meal, we returned to the television room and the rest of the patients started getting ready for the bus that would take them to an AA meeting. I was told I would have to stay behind with Tony and Jill because we would need further medication and the bandages on my wrists needed changing. I was allowed to go to bed; there was a curious comfort and security in knowing that I was being watched at all times.

Attending AA meetings was part of the treatment. The first time I went to a meeting I was very cynical. They took a coachload of us from the unit to a meeting in Croydon. As I got off the coach and we made our way into the church hall where the meeting was being held, I was met by a well-dressed man. He must have been in his late-forties or early-fifties; he stuck out his hand and said, in a well-spoken voice, "Welcome. I'm Harry". We shook hands. I looked at him sceptically: how would someone like him have anything in common with someone like me?

Harry showed us into the main hall where the meeting was going to be held. The people in there all looked surprisingly normal, well-dressed, and they were laughing. Harry got two cups of tea and invited us to sit with him. He passed me a cup; he told me that he was an alcoholic! I remember thinking, "You don't have to lie to me mate; of course you're not an alcoholic. For a start, drinkers don't dress and talk like you." I then asked him how long he had been without a drink. He told me five years. I thought he was having a laugh — if someone was an alcoholic there was no way they could keep away from a drink for more then fives minutes, let alone five years. I was looking at him in total disbelieve.

When the meeting started, there were two guys sitting at the top table. One of them called the meeting to order and said, "Good evening, my name is Michael and I'm an alcoholic." Everyone in the room said, "Hi Michael." Then he introduced the speaker for the evening, Ian. Then Ian introduced himself in the same way and got the same response. He spoke for about half-an-hour; his story was almost identical to mine. He talked about how drinking had taken him to prisons, caused him to sleep rough and to beg. I was transfixed.

After he had finished, Michael threw open the meeting for people to speak from the floor. There were a lot of people in the room; one-by-one, in a refreshingly honest way, they shared stories about their drinking and what it had done to their lives. Then at the end of the meeting we all stood up and were invited to hold hands and say the "Serenity Prayer". I felt quite embarrassed standing there holding Harry's hand and the guy's hand on the other side of me.

And that was it. I thought that this was some sort of religious movement or cult and that I wasn't going to have anything to do with it, thank you very much. Harry gave me his phone number and told me that I could call him at any time.

After ten painful days, the medication had been gradually reduced to zero and I was now completely clear of all substances for the first time in years. I was still in the observation room. It was early June, around five in the morning. There was an absolute stillness in the air. The unit was completely silent; it would be another couple of hours before Pinel House would start to come to life when the day staff arrived. My bedroom overlooked a green field and I lay in bed gazing at the sunrise. I was awake early as I had had a restless night and my mind had been troubled. I had spent most of the night drifting in-and-out of sleep.

The realisation dawned on me that I was at the end of the road. I could no longer live and yet I did not have the courage to kill myself. As I lay in my hospital bed, waves of despair washed over me. The ghosts from the past came to haunt me and my mind became filled with terror, bewilderment, frustration, and despair. What was to become of me?

From my window, I watched the sun rising behind a row of trees at the end of the field. A slight wind bent the long grass towards me. It was then that I had a light bulb moment; it was some sort of an epiphany and my mind's eye was at long last opened. Up until that moment, my mind had been like an old dark attic that had become damp and dingy. There was just a single dim light bulb hanging down in the middle, barely illuminating the dark unseen corners and the old sacking lying on the floor with menacing things moving beneath it.

My mind was now a brightly lit room with no hidden, dark corners. A new world of consciousness and understanding opened-up to me, followed by a great feeling of peace. I knew that no matter how wrong things seemed to be at that moment, from now on everything would be alright. I realised at that precise moment that I had a choice: I didn't have to live this way. It was clear to me, and it was like putting the last two pieces into a jigsaw puzzle: I could see the whole picture.

I could choose *not* to drink and *not* to use alcohol if I wanted to; there was nothing in this world that could stop me. I realised that ninety percent of what I do is choice; the other ten percent is what happens to me. Sure I didn't have a particularly good start in life, but I can choose how I am going to react to life. Clearly, up until that point, I had chosen to respond to life in a negative way. After twenty years of substance abuse my ability to choose had diminished with every drink or pill that I had taken. I had been given the ability to choose and I knew that I did not need to take another drink or drug if I chose not to.

Not knowing exactly what had happened to me, I knew one thing for sure: I was determined not to take a drink or drugs again on daily basis. Just as I had been told at the AA meetings that I should live my life one day at a time, all I needed to worry about was not drinking today and let tomorrow take care of itself.

When this light bulb moment had faded, I just lay there in bed. There had been a paradigm shift in my mind — only a small one, granted, but I had started to think in a different way. I had a long way to go, but I had started to move in the right direction.

My thoughts were broken with the door of my room being opened. It was Les, the night nurse. He had a mug of tea in his hand. "I saw that you were awake so I've brought you some tea; also we will be moving you into the main part of the unit this morning," he said.

That simple act of kindness meant so much to me. I've learnt over the years that it's not necessary to do big things for people; it's the small things we do that can have such a big impact. Just by Les bringing me that tea, it showed me that someone was thinking about me.

That night at the AA meeting I made up my mind that, whatever it took to achieve what those people had done, I would do my upmost to try and do it. I sat there intently listening, soaking up every word like a sponge. That was another change. I would normally just sit there, mentally assassinating them, thinking that they were just a bunch of losers. I was now coming round to the idea that it might be me that was the loser. These people had what they wanted: they were sober and happy. I was far from being happy.

However, my biggest stumbling block was the concept of a God that they called a "Higher Power". Every now and again I would run into Harry at the different meetings we were taken to; I felt sorry for him because all he seemed to be doing was going to meetings. He didn't seem to have anything else in his life. He would sit down with me and talk about the programme. I told him my concerns about the God bit; he told me that I should try to keep an open mind and in time it would all fall into place.

As I began to feel physically better, I had a desire to join the elite or in other words "the Group". However, I was convinced that Dr Gayford would not allow someone like me on that programme. At the time, the Group was made up entirely of professional people such as a doctor, a vicar, a police officer, a nun, a chief nursing officer and an accountant. As part of the therapy for each of the Group's members, they would be required to write an abridged version of their life story; I perceived that as being a major stumbling block for me. I could just about put two sentences down on paper—how on earth was I going to do something like that?

The fear of returning to the outside world, however, motivated me to ask the staff if I could apply to go into the Group. I was told that my application would be considered, but I knew that there was only one vacancy and there were other patients who also wished to join it. I was convinced that I would not stand a chance of getting a place.

On Thursday mornings, Dr Gayford would interview potential candidates to assess their level of motivation. Jill, another woman and I were told that Dr Gayford would be seeing us. I was the last one to be interviewed. He asked why I wanted to go into the Group; I told him that I felt it had a lot to offer me. He asked what contribution I could make; I told him that I did not feel that I had much to offer. He then said that he felt that I could make an enormous contribution to the Group. I did not have a clue what he was talking about. He told me that I had been picked to join.

I sat there with my mouth open, hardly able to believe it. I felt a rush of panic come over me as I hurriedly said, "But I can't spell; how will I be able to write my life story?" For the first and only time in my entire relationship with the doctor, he smiled broadly and said, "Bob, I want to let you into a secret: I can't spell either. I am sure you will be fine." With that he showed me the door. I walked slowly to the television and sat down to recover.

That small achievement was my first taste of success that was not connected with criminal behaviour. I had actually gone for something and got it. I sat there stunned. I could hear Jill, who was getting abusive with the staff and was threatening to have a drink if she was not allowed to stay in the unit, but the commotion passed over me. My thoughts were broken by a nurse who came to congratulate me and to tell me that I would be moving over to the Group's wing after lunch on Sunday.

On the following Saturday — 20th June 1981 — a seemingly small event occurred in my life: a young woman came to the unit to give a presentation. It was a morning like any other; no warning bells rang to tell me that that day would be significant. Then the most beautiful young woman I had ever seen in my life walked into the room. Apart from her obvious beauty, there was something very special about her. I could not put my finger on what it was. She introduced herself as Sue and gave an inspirational talk about her life problems. She was well-equipped to do so: she had also suffered for a long time with life-controlling challenges. She told us how she was coping with life and how she had managed to put her problems behind her. She also talked about the importance of developing a spiritual side to our nature. Something in the way she spoke about her relationship with God struck a deep chord within me, and when she left I could not get her out of my mind.

The following day I moved into the Group's accommodation. It was my thirty-seventh birthday and all my worldly possessions fitted into a small bag. The unit was empty as the Group's members had gone home for the weekend.

By late afternoon the members were drifting back. Their spouses were dropping them off; they all seemed to be affluent and had new cars and were well-dressed. I felt so inferior. These people seemed to have so much more going for them.

Following the in-house AA meeting, I sat in the Group's sitting room and we started to make our acquaintances. It was soon clear to me that, just like prison, there was a pecking order. Peter was a vicar and, like the other members of the Group, was in his early-forties. He had been given the job of "group leader" by the staff, which meant that he was the spokesperson for the group.

Peter had been admitted to the unit on the advice of his bishop, as his drinking was out of control. The story goes that at a funeral service, a bit for worse for drink, he started to recite the wedding ceremony! Then there was Linda, the police officer. Her job was assistant group leader. She had found the pressure of police work too much and had started drinking as a result. Before long it had got out of control, leading to a suicide attempt by carbon monoxide poisoning.

Michael was a doctor. He was the editor of the Pinel House magazine and had been arrested for drink driving. His marriage was on the rocks because of his abuse of alcohol. Then there was Mary who was a nun. She was the assistant editor of the magazine and was a lace curtain drinker, i.e. someone who would keep up a front of respectability, but would always be drinking behind closed doors. The other group members would joke and say that her drinking had become a "habit"! Next there was Richard; he was the accountant. He was in charge of the social committee for the Group. Members had to host a reunion once a month for former patients and their families; it was down to Richard to coordinate the event. He was in his last week of the Group; I didn't find out about him or his drinking. Last, but by no means least, there was Noreen, the chief nursing officer and a secret drinker. She was taking over from Richard as the reunion coordinator.

Then there was me, a former prisoner and down-and-out. What a combination we made! I am convinced that Dr Gayford had a strange sense of humour by putting me in among the comfortably well-off, middle-class professionals. I felt like a fish out of water and terribly inferior. I had nothing in common with these people. Peter, I know, had a big problem with having a criminal around. The other members possibly had problems sharing their personal lives with someone like me, but they were able to hide their feelings.

The following morning, I was given one of the Group's tracksuits to wear. It was like a badge that distinguished us from the rest of the patients; it was also a great leveller because we were all dressed the same. Within a few days, and with a great deal of help from Linda, I managed to make a start on my life history.

After my first two weeks, I was allowed to go home for the weekend. When I returned to the group and told the other members that I had spent the weekend at AA meetings, someone would raise their eyebrows as if to say, "Don't you get enough of that stuff in here during the week?" Peter would voice his disapproval by saying things like, "I would have thought you would have had better things to do with your time." This was a turning point in my life as the people pleaser. I had discovered within myself, to my great surprise, a wellspring of courage to do what I felt was right. I no longer cared what Peter thought about my attending meetings at the weekend.

Five weeks into the programme, Linda had typed up my life story and it was my turn to go through it with the staff and the other members of the Group. This process would take place over a period of four days. The person in the "hot seat" would be grilled for an hour each day about their life. I started to read my story out loud, painfully slowly. When I got to the point where my father died, I started to cry uncontrollably; all the feelings I had been blocking for years gushed out. The little boy inside of me was crying out for help. It was in that hospital room with my fellow alcoholics that, some twenty-seven years after his death, I was allowed to mourn my father's passing and the healing began. After all that time I began to realise that it was not my fault that he had taken his life. I realised that at that time I had only been a small boy and not the monster I perceived myself to be for all those years.

We then moved on to talk about the breakdown of my marriage. I told them that it was entirely my fault that the marriage had ended in divorce. I was told that it was a partnership and the blame was not all mine. They pointed out to me that when Pam and I first met, I had just come out of prison. I was drinking and taking drugs nearly all of my waking moments, and I was financing my drug habit through crime. I agreed that that was true. Then I was asked, "Would you want to marry someone like that?" I answered, "No, of course not!" It was pointed out to me that Pam might have had a problem herself by wanting to spend her life with someone like me and that our relationship was doomed from the start.

Thursday afternoon came round when Dr Gayford would sit in on the Group and pull together all that had been discussed over the four days. I had already witnessed such sessions when he summed up other people's lives. He was a wordsmith; he was gifted with the use of language. He would launch into a long discourse, using words I had never heard before. As someone who has dyslexia, I have a tremendous problem with pronunciation and I have always admired people with the gift of language.

After the doctor had listened to the report from the Group and the staff on my life history, he turned his attention on me and with a piercing stare that pinned me to my chair he said, "Bob, I feel that you are institutionalised. You are now using hospitals rather then prisons. You are at the crossroads of your life. If you continue to drink and take drugs, you will end up an inmate in some long-term institution. The choice is yours: either you stop abusing substances, or you will end up in places like this for the rest of your life." And with that he got up and walked out with the staff trailing behind him.

I took myself off to my room, disappointed and angry. Where was the flowery language, the inspiring messages that had so characterised his pronouncements on other people? I felt that he had got it wrong in my case. I was not institutionalised. Then I honestly asked myself, "What would happen if I were told to leave this hospital tonight?" The truth of the matter was that I would not be able to cope. His words echoed in my head, as had the words from the Salvation Army lady four years earlier. She had said much the same thing when she had asked me how old I was. My mind ached with trying to come to terms with this new knowledge. Was it possible that they were right and I was wrong? Had I really become *that* dependent on places like this? Was this it for me? The old despair swept over me briefly, only to be replaced by a feeling of determination. He was right: I *was* institutionalised but I was also developing the tools of self-awareness and courage, as stated in AA's prayer. The fact that a prayer, albeit in poem form, was being a source of comfort to me did not seem as alien as it had previously.

Chapter 8

We can't change the life that we lived, but we can change the life we're living

Anonymous

I threw myself into group therapy and the AA meetings. I was hungry to find out how to keep away from drinking, and had even started to think that there might be something beyond it all; someone or something that was watching over me. Without doubt my life was slowly changing—was it possible that there was a God who cared for and loved me? Surely not—this was against everything I had ever believed, and yet my heart was softening towards the idea.

Life in Pinel House continued and my self-awareness grew. It had been a few weeks since I had been through my life history; Peter, Linda, and Michael had gone home and there was a whole new group forming. The staff had made me group leader and I went on a bit of an ego trip thinking that I had cracked it and that they had seen something special in me—it wasn't until I was having a chat with another patient who commented that I had been made "Chief Loony" that I was cut down to size!

My time at Pinel was coming to an end and I was getting a little concerned that my three months would soon be up. I felt that I was nowhere near ready to face the world.

The staff had arranged hostel accommodation for me, but I would need to go for an interview to see if I was suitable to live there. I caught the bus to the hostel and met the warden, who was a warm and friendly person. She told me that it was a dry house. Most of the other men in the hostel were former patients of Pinel House. She told me that she would let me know within the next few days if she could offer me a bed.

True to her word, she phoned a couple of days later to offer me a place. By late-August 1981, I was getting ready to face the outside world, sober for the first time in a long time. It was just a few days before my discharge when I received a phone call from Brendon, a guy I had met at AA meetings. He'd been sober since Moses was a boy, so he'd been around for a bit! My ego was boosted by his call—I thought that he had also seen something special in me. However, the reason for his phone call was to see if there was anything he could do to help me. He knew that I would be discharged soon and was offering lifts to the meetings if I wanted them. I wanted to talk about the programme with him; I said that I was having a problem with the first step ("We admit that we are powerless over alcohol and that our life has become unmanageable"). I said to him, "I admit I'm powerless over alcohol, but I can't see where my life is unmanageable." It went quiet on the other end of the phone for a few seconds; then Brendon said, "You're talking to me from a nut house!" It had never occurred to me that normal people didn't come into places like this.

It was the Friday before the August Bank Holiday. I found myself saying goodbye to the staff and the friends I had made in Pinel. A lot of the people felt sorry for me seeing that I didn't have a home or relationship to return too. I did not see it that way at all: the majority of people I had met in hospital were leaving to go and sort out damaged relationships; their careers were in tatters; they would have to face all those problems the moment they were discharged. Well, in my case, all I had to do from now on was work on me. The only way for me to go was up.

I left Pinel House with my small bag of clothes and a few pounds in my pocket. I was ready to take on the world. I made my way to the hostel in Norwood, South-West London; not too far from my old friends, but far enough away so that I would not keep running into the people I used to drink with. I settled into the hostel, and soon had found a few days work with my old mate Mickey Bradford. I didn't need a lot of money; just enough to pay to my rent and the bus fares to meetings. With any that was left over, I would buy clothes.

A few weeks later in mid-September, I passed my driving test — the first test I had ever succeeded at! The sense of achievement was incredible. I have Michael and the other group members to thank for encouraging me to take it. One day, in a group session, I was complaining about the fact that I was not even a qualified driver and for years had been driving illegally. It was then that Michael and the others suggested that it might be a good idea if I took a driving test. It never occurred to me to do something positive; to actually do something about it instead of just complaining. They were right!

By October, I had managed to get a job driving a van. This opened-up a whole new world to me and took me all over the country. I visited places that I had only seen on television. In all my thirty-seven years, I had not ventured much outside South London and I loved the freedom the job gave me.

I ran into Sue one evening at a meeting. She remembered me from Pinel House and we had a long conversation about how life was treating me now. She gave me her phone number and told me that I could phone her at anytime if I was struggling. I felt like a schoolboy — shy and tongue tied — because she was so attractive.

After a short while I found a whole new circle of friends surrounding me in the fellowship and that life was taking on a whole new meaning. I struck up a friendship with a wonderful man by the name of Andrew. He had been sober for about eighteen months and he too was a former patient of Pinel House. I would often go to meetings with him and we would talk on the phone.

As time passed, I was feeling concerned about my mental state. I was having violent mood swings: one minute I was laughing and joking; the next I was depressed. I was worried that I might be bipolar like my dad. I had been self-medicating with alcohol and drugs for so many years; was it only now, now that I wasn't using, that my true personality was coming through? I told Andrew about my concerns; he told me that most people go through this sort of behaviour after years of substance abuse. He reassured me that what I was experiencing was quite normal for people like us. I asked him what had helped him get through this; he told me he had received a lot of comfort from praying. I thought, "What on earth is he talking about? Here am I with a *real* problem and all he can do is talk about praying!" I told him that I couldn't see how prayer would help my situation. He told me to try it, and, tongue-in-cheek, I said that I would.

A few days went past and the mood swings were happening again. My thoughts went back to the conversation I had had with Andrew about praying; I thought that it couldn't do me any harm, so I gave it a try. I did not have a clue how to pray! One evening, in the privacy of my room, I knelt by my bed. Although it was about eleven-thirty in the evening and I was on my own, I still put the side of the bed cover over my head just in case someone could see me. I did not know what to say; I just whispered, "Will Andrew's God please help me?" Nothing happened. I did not feel anything and there was no blinding light — other than that I was acting like a complete Muppet kneeling there!

The next day I phoned Andrew and told him that I had been praying and that nothing had happened. He asked me how many times I had tried; I told him once. He suggested that I should try it several times before I knocked the idea of praying; he said, "If you can't make it, then fake it." After that, I prayed each morning and asked some unseen and unknown being to help me stay sober for that day; each evening, I would thank Him for helping me keep my sobriety. I still did not have any idea of what I was praying to.

The fellowship was having a convention at Cane Hill Hospital, one of the institutions I visited with my father when I was a small child. However, this time was different. As I walked up that same drive with Andrew in the warm autumnal sunshine, I felt that a lot of ghosts from my childhood had been laid to rest. I was no longer that frightened little boy anymore; I was a grown man, and after years of enslavement by the events of my childhood, I was consigning most of them to history and moving on in life.

As we walked into the main hall, there were hundreds of people mingling around. From out of the crowd Sue appeared looking absolutely gorgeous. She was wearing a light blue outfit; with her long blonde hair resting on her shoulders and the sun shining from the window onto her, she looked angelic. She was selling raffle tickets. Once again I was bowled over by this woman. We bought some tickets and Andrew made arrangements with Sue for the three of us to have lunch together. Then we took our seats.

I had never been to a convention before. Harry, the man who spoke to me at my first meeting, was on the stage and his job was to introduce the speakers. He stepped up to the podium and opened the convention by thanking all of us for coming. Then he introduced the first speaker. As the person stepped up to the microphone, I thought to myself that maybe in five years or so I might be asked to speak at a convention. I began to feel nervous at the thought of talking to so many people; then it occurred to me that I didn't have to worry about that today — it would be years before they asked me to do anything like that.

I was carried away with the spirit of the occasion. Some of the speakers were like stand-up comedians — they were so entertaining. They spoke about what alcohol had done to their lives. Laughter is a great healer: once we have the ability to laugh at ourselves, we can then start to forgive ourselves.

Lunchtime came around. I eagerly set off with Andrew to join Sue. We sat on the lawn eating our picnic and enjoying each other's company when Harry joined us. We all shook hands and then he asked Andrew if he could talk to the conference for ten minutes that afternoon. Andrew's face went white: he had never spoken at a convention before. However, after a lot of cajoling from Sue and Harry, he agreed to do it.

I just sat there thinking how on earth could anyone stand up at short notice and talk to an audience of that size. Then Harry interrupted my thoughts. "Bob, I would like you to talk for ten minutes also." Completely shocked, I said, "I can't speak in front of all those people! Anyway, I have only been around for a few months. What could I talk about?" He replied, "I have heard you speak at meetings. Your gratitude for being sober has always come across so strongly. Just talk about your gratitude." I sat there lost for words. Then Andrew's voice broke the deadly silence: "He would love to do it, Harry." Thanks for nothing, Andrew!

Harry said, "Good. I would like the pair of you to meet me backstage ten minutes before the afternoon session starts." With that he walked off, and I spent the rest of lunchtime in a state of shock. Sue was lovely; she was so reassuring and told me that I would be fine.

I did not eat much after that. Before I knew it, Andrew and I were backstage at the allotted time to be met by Harry, who introduced the four other speakers, all of whom had been sober for years. What was I doing with these people? I became weak at the knees thinking about it. It was agreed that Andrew would talk first and then I would follow him. We took our places at the table on the stage. I felt quite sick as I looked over the sea of faces in front of us. Before I knew it, Andrew was finished. Then I was introduced. I walked up to the podium and looked out at the audience.

Sue was sitting in the front row. She smiled at me reassuringly. I took a deep breath, said a quick prayer, then began, "Good afternoon, my name is Bob and I am an alcoholic." The whole audience came back with, "Hi Bob." I started by talking about my life's path and the long road that I had trodden to bring me to that moment in time. I finished with tears in my eyes, expressing my gratitude to the audience for helping me remain clean and sober. I said, "It was in rooms like this and with people like you that I was allowed to climb out of the gutter with dignity. I thank you from the bottom of my heart." I finished on ten minutes dead. As the applause rose, I felt that I belonged to a whole new family. Those people out there had been where I had been, in pits of despair, and we had all lived to tell the tale.

That was my first attempt of public speaking. Little did I know that the day would come when I would speak in places like the House of Lords and Eton College, and would be on the after-dinner circuit. I would also give lectures in universities and colleges throughout England. I would get involved on the international speaking circuit, giving presentations in Europe and America as well as appearing on television and radio. However, all this was far from my mind as my eyes were once again drawn back to Sue, who was smiling at me from the audience and applauding. She winked at me — my legs turned to jelly!

A couple of weeks later, I bought a Volkswagen Beetle, allowing me to pick up people and take them to meetings. One evening, I saw Sue at a meeting and asked her if she would like a lift home. She said she would love one. On the drive to her flat, I found out a little bit more about her. She was a single mother who had a two-and-a-half-year-old daughter, Charlotte, and was currently dating someone else. From then on I would pick her up a couple of times a week and go to a meeting with her.

By January 1982, I had moved out of the hostel into my first flat. Living on my own was a first for me. I was in a large old Victorian house that had been converted into small apartments. Mine had little furniture; the living room was too small and the bedroom was too large. I would go to meetings complaining that the person who converted the house into flats must have had a drink problem because of the way the place was laid out.

One evening, Andrew came back to have a look. He was in there all of thirty seconds when he said, "Move the furniture around — you are living in the wrong rooms!" Just before I moved in my landlord had decorated the bedroom, so the bed had been left in the living room. Now, I'm no fool — if there is a bed in the room, it must be a bedroom! I was so institutionalised from being in prison, where we would never move anything around in our cells, I had not developed much in the way of creative thinking!

Life was continuing to go well, and as each new day came I was gaining an inner-strength that I never thought was possible. My family, although pleased by the change in me, were confused by the new "Bob", and my brothers and I were becoming estranged by the differences in our value systems. I would try to talk about my beliefs, but since I was not sure exactly what it was that I believed in, this just caused more confusion. Their attitude was, "Well, if it keeps him off the drink and out of prison, it must be harmless. Poor old Bob — he's got some sort of religion now!" The change in my attitude unsettled my family and friends from my former life, and their emotions ranged from contempt to pity.

There was still a large stumbling block for me: the unresolved situation with my former family. Unbeknown to me, Pam and the boys, along with her new husband, had moved into the same area where I lived, having moved away from our old home in the hope that I would not find them once I was released from prison.

One morning, as I was leaving my flat, I discovered Pam standing at a bus stop near to where I was living. She almost passed out when I approached her. I tried to put her at ease; I attempted to reassure her that it was alright and that I didn't wish her any harm. I tried to apologies for the way I had behaved in the past, telling her that I was a changed man. I fear that little got through to her; she was understandably too nervous to take in what I was trying to say.

As time went by, I would see David and Paul near the local shops. I wanted so much to talk to them; I was so near, yet so far away. They had a new life in which I had no part to play. While I was glad to see them, I just wanted to find a big hole and bury myself in it. How could I have just walked out of their lives? In the grim light of utter sobriety, the enormity of what I had done began to dawn on me: I had swapped my sons for a bottle and some pills. My heart ached and the only comfort was in the meetings, where I would hear other stories like mine and we would try and help each other. However, real comfort was elusive, and I recognised that because of my actions I would have to live with some measure of regret for the rest of my life. There were times when I would feel like giving-up and the old feelings of worthlessness would swamp me.

One night I was at home when I received a call from a local hospital. Mary, the Nun, had been admitted for drinking again and was going back to Pinel House. She had asked for me to take her there, so I got into my trusty Beetle and set off for the hospital in near blizzard conditions. When I got there, Mary was so drunk she could hardly stand. We managed to get her in the back of the car and headed slowly towards Pinel. The closer we got, the more rural it became and the more difficult the roads were to drive on. By now Mary had started to sing at the top of her voice, giving me a rendition of *You'll Never Walk Alone*. I tried to approach Pinel by the hill, but even with my back wheel drive VW the road was impossible. I had to go by another route which was much longer and slower. Mary was sobering up and had stopped singing; now she was getting depressed to the point where she was contemplating suicide. I thought, "Why me? Why am I stuck in a blizzard with a half-drunk, suicidal nun?!"

We eventually arrived at Pinel. I managed to get Mary safely admitted and made my way home before the weather closed in. As I drove, I thought about what my previous lifestyle had to offer and had to admit to myself that, despite the pain of facing old behaviours, this new life was the only one I wanted to live. Mary's "slip" had served to remind me of the first priority in my life: not to take a drink.

Spring arrived and I was getting more and more involved in the fellowship. I began attending other meetings to ask people to come and talk at mine. I also got involved with the telephone service, answering calls at the central London call centre. My shift was from two to six pm on a Sunday afternoon. People would phone up out of sheer desperation, wanting to stop drinking. I would try to encourage them to let me send someone round to talk to them. There were also the ones that were suicidal, and I would do my best to talk them down. And then there were the ones who would hang up—I was never sure what happened to them. I would go off duty completely drained, but somehow refreshed. I knew that the time spent working with others helped me to function better as a person.

Another way I could help others was by having my name put on the call-out list. If someone living in my area called in and needed a visit, I would be contacted and asked to go and see them. On one occasion I received such a call; I set off with another member to see what we could do to help. All we knew was that the man's name was Ron. We arrived at the address; his wife opened the door and showed us into the lounge, where Ron was sitting. He was shaking from head-to-toe—he hadn't had a drink that day. We told him about the fellowship and how it had helped us to stop drinking. All the time he was staring at me. Now and again he would say, "Don't I know you?" I said, "Maybe". He did look familiar, but I could not place him. Then, after about twenty minutes, Ron said, "I know you. You used to be in Brixton Prison." "That's right," I replied. Then it dawned on me where I knew him from: he used to be my landing officer. What a reversal of roles! We managed to get Ron to his first meeting and a short while after that he went into Pinel House. He soon retired from HM Prison Service and the last I heard he was living a happy and sober life.

As summer wore on, I was spending a lot of time with Sue. We would go to meetings together and by now her relationship with her boyfriend had finished. We had a real friendship; I had never had one like this with anyone, especially not a woman. However, I was aware that I had feelings towards her that were more then just friendship. I did not know what do; I knew that I would be punching above my weight; I thought that I stood no chance with a woman like that and was convinced that she liked me as a friend but nothing else. I thought that if I told her how I really felt about her she would end our friendship.

The only way I could deal with it was by cutting down the time I was spending with her. However, that never worked as I missed her too much. I kept telling myself to forget it; she would not want to have anything to do with someone like me. I was thirteen years older; she was privately educated and came from a middle-class background. I stood no chance. She was well out of my league. I wasn't prepared to ruin the good friendship we had by telling her about how I felt.

I decided to go to Spain on holiday. I thought that maybe I would feel better by being away from her. The night before I was due to leave, I called Sue to say goodbye. Something prompted me to say how I felt about her; I told her that I wanted to be more than just friends. There was silence down the end of the line for a few moments. My mind raced. I thought I had blown it.

Then her voice came back quietly down the line: "I feel the same way about you." I could not believe what I was hearing. I thought for one horrible moment that she was joking. She was not. We agreed that we would get together to talk about it when I got back from Spain.

The next two weeks were the longest of my life. I had gone on holiday with a friend from the fellowship. This was my first trip abroad, but all the wonderful sights and new experiences were lost on me because all I could think about was Sue. I was acting like a lovesick teenager and could not wait to get back home to be with her.

Chapter 9

The only talent I have is I can choose a good wife

Bob Turney

S ue and I went on our first date on Friday 13th August 1982. After that, we saw a lot of each other. I discovered that her parents were divorced and that her father had remarried; I also found out that she was a member of the Church of Jesus Christ of Latter-day Saints, better known as the 'Mormons'. I knew very little about them. What I did know was that they didn't drink or smoke — I found that out from a television programme I had watched about the Osmonds. Sue told me that she had not been attending church for some time and described herself as a "less active" member. However, her father and his new family were very much involved in the church.

On some weekends we would arrange for Charlotte, Sue's daughter, to stay with Sue's mum, and we would go away for the weekend. Once, whilst visiting Salisbury, we were walking around the beautiful cathedral, locked in a heavy discussion about the meaning of life. She told me what her beliefs were and they made prefect sense to me. I had been out of rehab for eighteen months and the way my life had gone since then was nothing short of a miracle; I had started to consider that there might be a God or a "Higher Power", as it was referred to in AA. While spending a lot of time looking at different religions, I had attended quite a few churches in the hope that I would find what I was looking for. However, nothing seemed to be right: the people I met were really warm and friendly, but it seemed to me that their God was putting everyone on guilt trips, and that just didn't feel right.

The feelings I had for Sue were nothing like those I had had for anyone before. However, I had just one big hurdle to overcome: I had to tell her that I was unable to read and write properly and I wasn't sure how she would react. As she came from a middle-class background, she had been privately educated and got a lot of pleasure from reading and going to the theatre. As for me, that wasn't my world — it was well outside the life I knew.

One evening, I plucked up enough courage and told her. I stood there trying to read the reaction in her face. She just threw her arms around my neck and said, "I love you for the person you are and not what you can do!" She made me feel twenty feet tall — she loved me for who I was.

That remark made me feel that I had some value in spite of my inabilities; it helped to bring my literacy problems into some sort of perspective. I started to understand that being unable to do something had little to do with the sort of person I was or the one I could become. My self-esteem grew just a little that day.

Up until that point, my life had been like a black and white negative — grey in parts — but Sue had brought colour and passion into my life. She is the sort of person that if you spend time with her, she would make you want to be a better person. As a matter of fact, she has been quoted on a number of occasions as saying that she found my dyslexia endearing, that it was one of the things that attracted her to me. Can you imagine how that made me feel? For years I had been living with a self-imposed label of inadequacy — as if that made me an idiot — but now there was someone saying something entirely different about me. Although I struggled to understand what she was implying, she had put a dent in the entrenched beliefs I had about myself — I began to see myself in a completely new light.

By now I was heavily involved with AA meetings and was doing a lot of work with the newcomers. It was a great joy to see them starting to rebuild their lives. I also started giving public information talks to all sorts of organizations, such as the police, magistrates, probation officers and judges. I felt that I was making a real contribution to the community in which I was living — unlike in my past life where the only contribution I made was to the crime statistics!

Ten months into our relationship, Sue announced that she was pregnant and we were both delighted with the news; a short while later I moved in with her and Charlotte. With the coming of the new baby it felt that I was being offered a second chance and that it was time to redeem myself for walking-out on my two sons. This time I was determined not to make the same mistakes again. I stopped smoking and I threw myself into the pregnancy. I went to pre-natal classes with Sue and followed the baby's development with great interest, sharing the joy when we saw the first scans. As time went by, Sue became more radiant and beautiful. I was starting to be more and more aware of the wonderful creation around me; I started to notice the trees and birds when I took Sue and Charlotte for walks in the park.

My relationship with my mum and brothers was improving. I had been sober for a little over two years, but they were still unsure how to react to me; they must have been thinking "how long was this new 'Bob' going to last." Who could blame them? They had had twenty years of me being drunk and going to prison, so I could understand their scepticism.

At the beginning of August, my mum's health declined. She was diagnosed with cancer. Mercifully, she died only a few weeks later in September. I visited her while she was in hospital and just spent time sitting with her. Her last words to me were, "Keep going to them meetings. They are doing you a world of good, son." The next day she died. At least I had had a couple of years getting to know her. I was so thankful that I wasn't in prison, or in the gutter drunk right up until she died. I was able to spend some time with her, trying to make amends for the way I had been in the past. In her own way she had been brave throughout her life and she set an example for me of being dignified in dying.

My brothers were sure that her death would start me off drinking again, but that was the last thing on my mind. After the funeral, I found that I was in an emotional turmoil: on the one hand, I was mourning the passing of my mum; on the other, I was looking forward to the birth of our child. I thought about life and death and spent a lot of time discussing mortality with Sue. She told me that Mormons believe life is eternal.

As the pregnancy moved on, Sue was growing more and more gorgeous by the day. There was something really special about her; I was absolutely besotted and still am. February 1984 saw the birth of our daughter, Sarah, who was the most beautiful baby I had ever seen. There were problems with the birth and she had to be delivered by caesarean section. There were also complications with the operation and the doctors told us that it would be most unlikely that Sue would be able to have any more children, which came as a shock to us both. We had been hoping to have a few more, but the important thing was that Sue and the baby were alright.

One evening, after we had put the children to bed, I asked Sue to marry me. It was something that I had been planning to do for a long time but had put it off because I knew that she would refuse! I was right. She said that she could not marry me because she would only feel right if she was married in the Mormon Church—anywhere else was not an option. However, she didn't feel right doing that because she had not been to church for years and would feel like a hypocrite. She said she knew that her logic was questionable, but that was how she felt. She said that she loved me and was committed to both me and the children, but marriage was out of the question.

I told her that I respected her wishes but vowed that I would marry her one day. That was what drove me on to ask Sue to marry me at every opportunity. I would even wake her up at two in the morning and ask her, hoping to catch her off guard!

Sue's father and his new wife Marian moved to Henley-on-Thames. Marian had four sons from a previous marriage and they both had two new children from their own marriage. Sue's dad invited us to bring the kids and to spend a day with him and his family. I felt a bit uncomfortable about going because I had only met Jim once before; I had not met his wife—she was getting over the death of her teenage son who had drowned in a horrendous swimming accident. I was really unsure about how to handle the situation, but they had extended their hand of friendship and we felt that we should go.

When we got there, they made us feel very welcome. I was deeply touched by Marian, who, when she talked about the loss of her son, demonstrated an absolute faith that she knew she would be reunited with him one day. It was one of the most moving conversations I have ever had—I had never witnessed so much faith. Here was a mother who only a few months previously had lost a child, but her faith was carrying her through the most horrific situation any parent could find themselves in.

After dinner that evening, Jim, Marion and I had a long discussion about the church. Sue could see where the conversation was going and that I had more than a passing interest. It concerned her as she felt that she was not ready to make a commitment to return, but events seemed to be overtaking her.

We returned home and life went on as normal. I carried on attending meetings and was still driving a van for a living. I got a lot of fulfilment out of being with Sue and the kids and would continue to ask her to marry me. I was still getting the same answer. I asked her why we could not get married in the Mormon Church; to my way of thinking, it would not matter if we didn't attend church afterwards. She told me that it was not as simple as that: her church was not like other churches where sometimes people would only attend for weddings and funerals. Being a member of her church meant commitment, and she was not ready to make that commitment yet.

Six weeks later, we received an invitation from Matthew, Sue's stepbrother, to his wedding. Sue was apprehensive about going because she had not been inside a chapel in years. Out of loyalty to her family, she reluctantly agreed to attend the service.

It was a warm September day, and as we drove out of London towards Reading, where the wedding was to take place, I could sense Sue's nervousness. As I walked into the chapel, I was struck by how friendly these people were. Within just a few minutes I could see the importance they placed on family relationships. I caught a small insight as to why Sue would want to be married in this church. People were so welcoming; there was something special about them that I just could not put my finger on. Whatever it was, I felt I wanted to know more about the church. The wedding service was different from anything I had ever experienced before; it was so warm, and the speakers talked about Matthew and his lovely young bride Rosie as if they loved them. I was so impressed with everything.

At the reception, Marion asked me how I liked the wedding. I told her that I thought it was wonderful. Then she asked me if Sue and I would like a wedding like that; I said that I would love one, but explained why I felt it was impossible. I told her of Sue's feelings about coming back to church and the fact that I felt that not being a member was a drawback. She then said something I did not quite understand at the time: "We're working on that!"

A couple of days after the wedding, I received a call from Jim inviting us to come down the following weekend. After lunch on the Saturday, we went for a walk down by the River Thames. Jim asked me what I thought of the wedding and how I liked the church; I told him that I was impressed with both.

In November, Sue and I were waiting at a railway station; we were going to visit her grandfather who was seriously ill. While we were on the platform, she said,

"You know that question you keep asking me?"

I was unsure what she was talking about.

"What question?"

"You know, the one you have been asking me all this time. Well, I've been thinking and the answer is yes."

I then realised what she was saying: she *would* marry me! I was the happiest man alive. We set the date for the wedding for the 29th December 1984. On the 1st January 1985, I was also baptised a member of the church.

We were married in Wandsworth Chapel, without a doubt one of the happiest days of my life. Sue's mum had the children while we went away for a few days. As I drove away with my new wife our route took us past Wanno. If someone had told me five years earlier when I was in there that in five years' time my life would be going in a whole new direction, I would have dismissed them as a lunatic — there was no way that was going to happen to me! But it did.

A short while later we discovered that Sue was pregnant again — so much for the doctors telling us we might not be able to have any more children! We were delighted with the news. Life for Sue and I had taken on a whole new meaning; we began to flourish and to feel that perhaps our major troubles were over and that we would continue without too much disruption to enjoy our peaceful existence.

As Sue's mum had lost three babies with heart defects, the doctors thought it would be a good idea for her to go for an in-depth scan. Afterwards, the specialist told us that the baby's heart was fine; he felt, however, just to be on the safe side, that we should go back in three weeks' time for a further scan, just to make absolutely sure. We were not concerned; we just thought that they were being over-cautious.

Three weeks later, we found ourselves back at King's College Hospital. This time the scan was done by a leading professor in fetal development. He seemed to take forever to complete his examination and then said the words that all expectant parents dread: "We have found some abnormalities with your baby." My heart sank; my head was spinning. I could not, would not, believe what I was hearing. He must be wrong. Not *our* child. I managed to focus on what he was saying: the baby had a hair lip and possibly a cleft palate.

Sue and I must have had a look of shock on our faces because he asked us if we had understood what he had just said. I broke the silence by explaining that my mother had had a cleft palate, which reinforced his prognosis. He said that he wanted to do more scans, but to wait for the baby to grow some more. So that they could do a more detailed examination, we were given another appointment in four weeks' time.

On the drive home, neither Sue nor I said very much. We were both feeling numb. The hospital had passed our names to a self-help group of people who had children with similar conditions. We had a phone call from a vicar who lived near us; he introduced himself as Jeffrey and said that he and his wife had eight-year-old twin boys, both of whom had cleft palates and hair lips. He invited us over to his home to meet his family.

When we arrived, they were most welcoming, supportive and understanding. Their sons had undergone corrective surgery and we were pleasantly surprised with the results. However, Jeffrey did warn us that when we first saw the baby it would have severe facial deformities. He showed us some photos of the boys before they had their surgery. We were quite shaken by them, but the whole point of the self-help group was to prepare us for when the baby was born.

By the time we were due to go back to the hospital, Sue and I had fully accepted that the baby would have a couple of problems; however, compared with the disabilities that some children are born with, a cleft palate and hair lip were minor and we knew that it could be corrected with surgery.

The professor did another scan and this time he took even longer than he had done before. He handed us the picture of our baby. To our untrained eyes it looked perfectly normal; however, he said, "I am sorry to tell you that the baby has an enlarged stomach." He went on to say that the baby would need surgery as soon as it was born, otherwise it would not be able to feed properly. As we were reeling from that news, he went on say that, in his opinion, the baby stood a sixty percent chance of having Down's Syndrome.

All I could hear was my heart thumping. The sweat ran down my back. I looked across at Sue who was in a state of shock. I wanted so much to put things right for her and take away the pain. I managed to turn my attention back to the professor who was saying, "You need to talk to one of my consultants. There are some decisions that we need to make."

With that, one of his assistants showed us into a small room and we were told that someone would be with us soon. We just sat there, holding hands, in a state of total shock. We hardly said a word to each other. I'm not sure how long we were in that room; it seemed only about ten to fifteen minutes and was certainly not long enough for us to gather our thoughts. Then the door opened and we were taken into a doctor's office. He briefly glanced at our file in front of him, then looked up and said, "The professor has explained that there are some problems with the baby?" "Yes", we said. He then started to talk about the quality of life the baby could be expected to have; in his opinion "it" would not have a very good one, but the choice of what to do was ours. Then he said, "If you choose to terminate this pregnancy it should be done as soon as possible."

We both told him that under no circumstances would we go along with his suggestion. We were immediately united in our decision. I had never had an opinion one way or another regarding abortion before, but now instinctively I knew that all life was sacred. Only a short while before they had given us a picture of our baby; now they were asking us to end its life.

He asked us why we were against termination; we told him that we felt we had no right to end a life. From our point of view, the baby would have two parents and two sisters who loved it. And no matter what problems we might have, we would somehow cope. He continued to question us about our religious beliefs for the next ten minutes. Our heads were swimming, yet he still kept bombarding us with questions about why we did not want to terminate the pregnancy. He finally agreed that whatever decision we made he would fully support us and help in anyway he could. He went on to say that he would like to perform an amniocentesis, which involved inserting a large needle into

Sue's abdomen and draining a sample of the amniotic fluid surrounding the baby. They could analyse the fluid to know for sure if the baby was suffering from Down's Syndrome. We asked how much of a risk it would be to the baby and were told that it was slight: one in every hundred would miscarry. We needed time to think about it and were told that we should come back to the hospital in a few days' time when we would be able to discuss our decision with the doctors.

I will never forget the drive home. We were shell-shocked. There was hardly any conversation; what we did say was on a superficial level. All we wanted to do was pick the kids up from the babysitter and to get home where we felt safe. We put the children to bed and spent the rest of the evening in a kind of stupor.

Later, in bed, the prayer I had said a hundred times at the end of AA meetings came into my mind. I knew that I had to accept the things I could not change—the baby's deformities—and knew I had to change the things I could. What I could change was my attitude. I was steeped in self-pity. If I started to forget about my needs and focused on helping Sue cope with this, I knew all would be well.

In our hearts we already knew that Sue would not be going through with the amniocentesis. We would not put our other children in a one-in-a-hundred risk situation. How could we do the opposite to our unborn baby?

Family and friends, both at church and from AA, were highly supportive. Within a couple of days we were back at the hospital telling the doctors that we did not want to have the amniocentesis. After that we would have to attend the hospital weekly so that they could monitor the baby's growth. Our weekly visits involved blood tests and further scans, and by now we could see the deformities—they could even measure the gap in the baby's mouth.

Each time we went to the hospital there seemed to be even worse news to contend with, as the specialists discovered that the baby had more disabilities than was first thought. On one occasion, we had a meeting with a doctor who had come to the conclusion that the baby could be so disabled that it would be in a vegetative state when born. He told us that he believed the baby might not survive long after birth, and if it did, it would need twenty-four hour care for the rest of its life. We would arrive home after those meetings with the doctors feeling exhausted from the emotional pounding we were getting.

It worried me that everyone was referring to the unborn baby as "it". So I temporally named the baby "Ron". Within a short space of time, the kids were calling the baby Ronnie Roo, and as time went by it was even shortened further to "Roo". Sue was growing more and more radiant and I could feel Roo kicking me in the back as we lay in bed at nights. One of the most wonderful things to come out of this whole experience was that Sue and I were closer in those dark days than we had been at any time during our relationship.

In one of the meetings with the doctors, it was decided that Roo would be delivered by caesarean section on the 27th June 1985. They told us that a bed would be provided for me in the Intensive Care Unit so that I could be on hand. They said that they would take a photo of Roo quickly, because their prognosis of the baby's survival was not good. However, if the baby did survive and was strong enough, it would be transferred to Great Ormond Street Hospital for Sick Children where an operation would be carried out on Roo's stomach. This would mean that Sue would be in one hospital and Roo in another on opposite sides of London — I would have to travel between the two.

The night before Sue went into hospital, we spent the evening together, not saying much; we knew that there would be lots of challenges ahead of us for the rest of our lives, but we could feel that we were united. Just because I was clean and sober it didn't mean that life was going to treat me any differently. I remember thinking, "Why me?" Then the thought came into my head, "Why not you?!"

The following day, I took Sue to the hospital. I spent most of it with her while some final tests were carried out; in the evening I went home to the children. As I put them to bed, we prayed that mummy and the baby would be alright.

I could not sleep much that night and the following morning found me back at the hospital. We were first on the operating list. I sat at Sue's bedside holding her hand; then they arrived to take us to the operating room and I was shown into a changing area where I put on a green gown and mask. When I got into the operating room, there were a lot of people milling around: surgeons, nurses, and paediatricians. I sat by Sue's side, grasping her hands as they started the operation. After what seemed a lifetime, someone announced that it was a girl and Roo started to cry. I turned around to see her for myself, but the paediatricians had her on the table in the corner. I could not see anything but doctors bent over examining her.

I started to walk over to them, but before I could get there one of the doctors said, "I cannot find any defects in this baby's mouth." From that moment I knew that Roo was a perfect baby. They said they had to rush her into intensive care where they would carry out more tests. With Roo in an incubator, we started for the door. I stopped to kiss Sue, who seemed once again to be in a state of shock; I told her I would be back as soon as I had the results, which I knew would be good.

Once in the Intensive Care Unit, it was not long before Roo was given the all-clear and was pronounced a perfectly healthy and normal baby! A nurse brought her to me and placed her in my arms for a cuddle, and as I held her I started to cry. The nurse put her arm around my shoulders; she too had tears in her eyes. Then I was passed a bottle and I gave Roo her first feed.

I made my way to the operating room. They had just finished cleaning-up Sue and were about to take her to the ward where Roo was waiting for us. The rest of the day was a total blur for me. I went home to begin telephoning people with the news that a miracle had happened. It took at least three days before I came back down to earth!

We renamed the baby Kate, although to this day everyone calls her Roo. Anyone visiting mother and baby could not fail to appreciate that something very special had happened. Sue seemed to radiate a bright light in the room. Cards and flowers poured in from well-wishers.

A few days later, I was making my way to the ward when I bumped into Jeffrey, the vicar who had been so supportive to us during the pregnancy. He was on his way to see Sue and asked how things were. In a strange way I felt guilty telling him that the baby was alright. Of course he was delighted with the news and asked me what I thought had happened. I told him it had to be some sort of a miracle. He looked at me dubiously as if he thought the experience had been too much for me; however, I knew then and I still know now that the age of miracles is with us—I only have to look at the events in my life to know that.

The professor also paid Sue a visit. He was puzzled as to what had happened. He told her that there were some things which medical science just cannot explain and this was one of them.

A few days after Roo was born, I was making my way up to the ward and ran into the doctor who had advised termination. We shook hands; I simply said that things had turned out much better than any of us had expected.

Within a week or so, Sue and the new baby were home and family life started to get back to normal. In a short space of time, the memory of what had happened started to fade.

My father-in-law offered me job working for him, which meant that we would have to move away from the London area to Reading in Berkshire. We rented a cottage in a hamlet just outside of the town called Gallows Tree Common. It was a lovely rural place and, after living in London, we found the environment hard to adapt to. However, I got involved in the local AA meetings; there was no shortage of friends.

Soon afterwards, Sue announced that she was pregnant yet again—great news! In September that year a stunning red head entered our lives. We had another daughter and named her Elizabeth—that name stayed for just one day before it became "Libby". By then I had reached the stage where I thought I could not have any more love for the children than I already did; but when Libby arrived, I discovered that I had even more to give.

Chapter 10

Differences create the challenges in life
that open the door to discovery

Anonymous

In the late-1980s, through my involvement with AA, I came into contact with our local Probation Service and was asked if I wanted to do some voluntary work for them. I jumped at the opportunity and was assigned to work with Roger, a probation officer. When I first met him he was running alcohol study groups. These were for people who had been convicted of alcohol-related offences and were placed on probation on the condition that they would attend one of these groups. The aim of the group was to try and educate people concerned about the damage their drinking could inflict on them, their families and the public in general.

From the moment I went into my first group I came to life — I just loved the work. One evening after a group session, I was sitting with Roger discussing the group and he asked me if I had ever considered becoming a probation officer. I thought that he was completely mad, or on crack, or something. I had a criminal record that made the Artful Dodger look like a choirboy and I could barely read and write — surely these couldn't be qualifications to become a probation officer. Now that I have been one I realise that I was overqualified!

Roger and I became friendly and I invited him and his wife over for dinner. Before they arrived, I told Sue that he had suggested that I should become a probation officer; I said it jokingly, but to my surprise she said, "That sounds like a good idea to me. You would make a great probation officer!"

Over dinner that evening, Roger again talked about me going into the Probation Service. As much as I liked the idea I just felt that it was out of my reach. I was not really convinced that I had the makings of the role. Roger and Sue suggested that I should at least consider it and explore the possibilities. I've always worked on the theory that if at least two people are saying the same thing they might have a point. I agreed that I would consider the idea.

By now Sue and I had set up a small catering business, which we ran from home. It was quite successful, but it was time-consuming and the children were not getting the attention that they needed. So we sold the business and I went back to the only way I knew how to make a living: driving. I drove a taxi for a while and then went back to driving vans. The work enabled me to support my family, but the voluntary work I was doing gave me far more satisfaction than the work I was paid for.

In May 1991, Sue announced that she was pregnant a further time. This was great news — it had been over four years since Libby was born.

I was still involved with Roger and the alcohol study groups and was also giving presentations on my life experience to local magistrates and other groups involved in the criminal justice system. These were always well-received. People would give me praise afterwards; I would cringe and think to myself, "If only they knew that I could not read or write properly, they would not be so keen to pay me compliments." I really did have a problem accepting any form of praise.

By October, I was unemployed. Sue was now eight months pregnant and I was feeling depressed. She sat me down and asked me what I wanted to do with my life. I told her that I would like to do some form of social work but felt it was impossible because I would need to get a qualification in the form of a university degree. "Well go for it then," she said. She went on to say that I needed to take time out and not to worry about getting a job. She suggested that I spend my free time exploring possible avenues to get some qualifications.

We decided that I would not work until the baby was born; instead I threw myself into my voluntary work with the Probation Service in the hope that it would help me gain a better understanding of the work I wanted to do and how I would get into it.

In November 1991, Sue gave birth to a boy. We could not believe it. After having four wonderful girls, we naturally assumed that we were going to have another girl, but we were blessed with a son who we named Joseph Robert Charles. For the next few months, I stayed at home with Sue and the new baby. Looking back on those days, they were some of the times when we were closest as a family.

I knew if I was going to stand the slightest chance of making any sort of career in social work, I would have to address the problem I had with dyslexia. I would have to get some sort of assessment so that the condition could be confirmed. I told my doctor about my problem and he referred me to a clinical psychologist. After a few tests, the psychologist confirmed that I was severely dyslexic. In fact, within a couple of weeks I was registered disabled because of it. I felt much better. Maybe I wasn't stupid after all.

My next step was to enrol on an education course. I found an adult college nearby and they were understanding when I told them about the problems I had with reading and writing and the bullying I had suffered at school. I had got into my mid-forties before I had had enough courage to try and tackle the problem head on. All through this, Sue was quietly encouraging me: when I would express doubts as to my abilities, she would make me feel that anything was possible and that I could achieve great things if I was prepared to work at it.

The professionals showed a lot of understanding. They tried to reassure me that they did a lot of work with those who had my disability and were aware of the problems faced by adults with dyslexia. First of all, they put me on a Basic English course. On my first day, I sat in my car outside the college, not wanting to go in. I felt a mixture of the old feelings of shame and guilt. I felt guilty: so guilty that I was not like other people and worried what they would think when they saw how bad my grasp of English really was. I was full of fear. I kept telling myself that I was a grown man and no-one could hurt me anymore, but still I had that same fear I felt all those years ago.

I plucked up enough courage to go in. As I walked through the gates my throat went dry; beads of sweat formed on my forehead and I was weak at the knees. I managed to overcome my fear and found my way to the classroom. My first day was a horrendous experience, despite the staff's attempts to put me at ease. However, after a few more sessions, I became more relaxed in the college environment. I was assigned to a volunteer named Dennis. He was a retired businessman and really helpful, taking me under his wing. Dennis and I would spend whole afternoons discussing the meaning of words and the use of language. I will always be grateful to Dennis: he gave me the confidence I needed to overcome the feelings of shame and fear.

By April 1992, I had been unemployed for eight months. The Probation Service had started to recruit staff for one of their bail hostels. I was encouraged by both Sue and Roger to apply for the job. I knew that my criminal record would no longer bar me from getting the job since I had volunteered for the Probation Service for almost three years — I could think of a thousand and one reasons why they would not employ me, but being an ex-con was not one of them.

I sent in my application form and was shortlisted for an interview. I discovered from Roger that I was up against some stiff competition for the job: fifty people had applied and they had whittled that number down to six. I was eventually interviewed by three senior probation officers. At the end of the interview I was told that they would contact me by phone by the end of the day and I would be told whether I had been successful or not.

When I got back home I tried to put the interview out of my mind. Sue asked how I thought it went; I told her that I did my best, but whether it was good enough to get the job I wasn't sure. Each time the phone rang I thought that it was the hostel calling — instead it would be a friend inquiring how I got on. As the day wore on, my confidence was starting to ebb. I convinced myself that I had made a good attempt, but the other candidates were stronger than me. It was almost six in the evening; by now I had convinced myself that I hadn't got the job. The phone rang. It was the hostel. I was told that I was the strongest candidate and they would like to offer me the job. I was shocked into silence; my head was swimming; I couldn't say a word. After a while, the voice on the other end of the phone said,

"Are you alright?"

"Yes, I'm a little shocked, that's all. I would love to accept the job."

The voice laughed.

"We will put confirmation in the post this evening; you should get it in a day or two. We will call you in few days to confirm your start date."

When I put the phone down, I wondered what on Earth was wrong with all the other candidates if they had offered me the job!

That was the start of my career with the Probation Service. I loved the work. They saw things in me that were far beyond my level of understanding; they gave me tasks that I thought were far beyond my abilities. But boy did I grow. Sure I made some mistakes, but what they were doing was getting me to reach inside of myself and to use the abilities I believed that I didn't have; I was discovering things within myself that I never thought existed.

For a year I was developing offending behaviour programmes. I got so much satisfaction out of it. I loved working with people like myself who were without hope and locked into negative behavioural patterns. As we worked with these people, we were sowing seeds that might not have borne fruit immediately, but that could in two months' or even five years' time make a real difference to their lives and that of their families.

By now I had come to the notice of the media. They found my story interesting and loved the idea of a "poacher turned gamekeeper". I was asked to do radio and television interviews and the press also wrote articles about me. I started advising television documentary makers on issues of law and order.

The Probation Service was very encouraging about my career development and I was advised that I should consider training as a fully-fledged probation officer. It is one thing to take a Basic English course but an entirely different thing to get a degree — just the thought of going to university was absolutely terrifying. Then it dawned on me that, after getting this far, the least I could do was to keep an open mind. I discovered that a local college had a one year part-time access course in social work. The objective of the course was to get mature students up to the academic level they needed if they wanted to apply for a place at university.

I applied and was offered an interview. There were thirty-five candidates and only twenty places. Straightaway I moved into negative mode, feeling that everyone there was far better than me. When the interviews were over they gave us some lunch; after lunch they were to tell us who had been selected.

I had lunch with the rest of the candidates and each one I spoke to seemed to have far more qualifications than I did — which is hardly surprising! That afternoon we sat around talking. Then my name was called and I was shown into the college principal's office. He invited me to sit down and then said, "We want to offer you a place on the course." My reaction was exactly the same as it was twelve years earlier in Dr Gayford's office at Pinel House. I told the principal, "I can't read or write properly. I don't think I will be able to cope with the course." He smiled and said, "I am sure you will cope perfectly well."

The Probation Service was great and allowed me time off to do the course. I started in September 1993 — once again the first few days were painful. Within a couple weeks we were given our first essay assignment. It was fifteen hundred words long and I was completely bowled over — the most I had ever written in my life had been a few letters. However, with the aid of a word processor and Sue as my proofreader I managed to do it. I got a reasonable grade for it as well. The sense of achievement I felt when I got the result back was wonderful. I had faced the fear of essay writing head on and got through it. After this, I started to concede that I might have a chance of going to university.

I got through the access course with flying colours; in fact I was named "Student of the Year". The tutors helped me put my application together for university and I applied to Oxford and Reading, being offered interviews for both. Although Oxford would have been the more prestigious university to attend, the course was not as good as the one being offered at Reading; therefore, I opted for the latter and grabbed their offer of a place with both hands.

As I was registered disabled, I was given a grant to buy a computer, and money was made available so that I could employ a proofreader. I was overwhelmed by the amount of help that was offered to me. I was told that the education system had let me down in the past and now they were trying to put things right. In all the years since I had left school, it never occurred to me that the system had let *me* down; I thought that I was the one that had let *them* down.

In October 1994, at the age of fifty, I embarked on my degree course. It was a journey of academic discovery for the next three years. I loved the classroom discussions. I would walk around the grounds on my lunch break, not believing that I was actually studying in such a place. The words of my friend Andrew from the AA meetings would come to mind: "Bob, never forget the wonderment of your recovery and always cultivate gratitude."

To subsidise my student grant, I worked in the probation hostel part-time. Part of my work was to organize groups for the residents. I invited guests in such as magistrates and police officers. I even wrote to a member of the House of Lords who was well known for his work as a penal reformer. Lord Longford had written many books on the subject and I asked him if he would come and talk about his work to the residents.

One afternoon, Sue received a telephone call from someone claiming to be Lord Longford. She thought that it was one of our friends having a joke and was just about to tell him that she was busy fixing a meal for the kids when she realised that this was no joke — this really was Lord Longford and he wanted to speak to me. She told him that I was not at home. I spoke to him later and made an arrangement for him to come and talk to the men in the bail hostel. It was agreed that I would drive to London and bring him to Reading.

I arrived at his Chelsea flat where he was waiting for me. I did not know how to address him and asked, "Do I call you 'My Lord', or 'Sir'? I am not sure!" He said, "'Frank' will do." On the drive to Reading, I told him about the hostel. Then he asked me to tell him a little about myself. When I finished, he told me that I should write a book. I thought that he was crazy. Me? Write a book? Who would want to read a book about me anyway? Not wishing to offend him, I told him that it was an interesting idea. We soon arrived at the hostel where he gave a wonderful presentation. On the drive back to London, he again suggested that I should write a book and I said that I would think about it. I dropped him off at the House of Lords, little knowing that over the years he would become a firm friend and his suggestion would set in motion a chain of events that would completely change the direction of my life once again.

A couple of days later, Frank phoned me, inviting me for lunch at the House of Lords. When I arrived he met me at the peers' entrance and showed me into the dining-room. Over lunch we discussed penal reform — that lunch lasted for four hours! He was again insistent that I wrote a book; again I promised him that I would think about it. Frank had a reputation for being a bit of an eccentric, and I treated his suggestion with the same dismissiveness as I had when Roger first suggested that I should go into the Probation Service. But with Frank's persistent encouragement I started on my first book, never believing that it would get published — who would want to read about me? I wrote the book while doing my degree; when it was written, I started to do media interviews, something that is common in my life now. A couple of days after the broadcasting of a television programme I had done about dyslexia, I was at my publisher's when he received a phone call from the BBC saying that there was a viewer who was trying to get in touch with me. It was my mate Terry. Later that evening, I phoned him and we had a two-hour catch up. We had both been convinced that the other one must be dead! He had gone AWOL after his girlfriend had left him, retreating into alcohol and drugs and ending up destitute in a Salvation Amy hostel in East London. This was almost the same time as I went into Pinel House, and he too whilst in the hostel had some sort of epiphany. He was now married with two sons. At the time I went to university, he had entered theology college and was now a minister of religion. We soon met up for a meal and have been close friends ever since.

I graduated from university with a 'Desmond' (two-two) in Forensic Social Work. On my graduation day, Sue and the kids were there with me. They watched me as I walked up to receive my degree from the vice-chancellor in my cap and grown.

Soon I started out as a probation officer. I worked at all levels of the service, with sex offenders, those with alcohol and drug issues, and supervising those on life licence (people who were serving life sentences, often for murder, who had been released back into the community). I also worked in prisons.

I was fifteen years clean and sober when my brother Fred became seriously ill with cancer. When I visited him, it was such a touching sight to see his wife and two kids caring for him as he was dying—he was just surrounded with love. About two weeks before his death, I paid him a visit. Carol told me that he was up in the bedroom. When I entered the room he was sitting on the edge of the bed looking out of the window. I sat beside him and put my arm around his shoulders; he rested his head on my shoulder. It was such an intimate moment, just like that evening, years earlier, after he had brought me home from the hospital, when I sat on his couch and he put his arm around my shoulders. I told him that I was sorry for all the problems I had caused him when I was drinking and that I should have been a better brother to him; he lifted his head off my shoulder, smiled, and said, "Thank you for being the brother you are now."

A couple weeks later he was admitted to a hospice. I went to see him. His wife and kids were at his bedside. They asked me if I would mind if they went for something to eat; I said of course not. I pulled-up a chair by his bed and sat there holding his hand as I talked about our life and family. After about an hour, we were joined by our two brothers, Tom and Stan, and all four of us sat around just chatting. When his family came back, we said our goodbyes and left. Fred died a few hours later.

My relationship with Frank Longford had grown and we started to attend functions together. One evening he offered me a job as his advisor for penal affairs, which I could combine with my probation work. When Tony Blair had his landslide victory in the 1997 General Election, and with Frank being a Labour Peer, a lot of doors opened for me. I was introduced to government ministers. I had meetings with Jack Straw, the Home Secretary — Jack even wrote a foreword to one of my books. I was also invited to No.10 Downing Street on a couple of occasions.

Frank was a bit of a loose canon. In debates in the Lords he would often shoot from the hip when making off-the-cuff speeches; so much so that when we were in his office there one morning, he received a note from Derry Irvine, the Lord Chancellor, suggesting that it might be a good idea if he were to prepare his speeches in future. When his secretary read the note to him, he thought for a moment; then he told me to write him a speech for the following day's debate on prisons. I told him that I couldn't do that because I didn't know the first thing about writing speeches. He simply said, "Of course you can, Bob," then went off for lunch.

For the rest of the day and well into the evening, I sweated over my laptop writing his speech. The follow morning I was in his office, and with the help of his secretary, who also proofread it for me, put the final touches to it.

Frank showed up at lunchtime and we went through to the dining-room. I went over the speech with him. The debate was due to start at three. I gave him the speech and he put it in his pocket; then we went into the chamber for the debate. When Frank's turn to speak came, he rose to his feet, didn't take the paper out of his pocket, and instead delivered another off-the-cuff address. Afterwards, I asked him why he didn't use my speech. He said, "I was only asked to have my speeches written. I wasn't asked to read them!"

Frank was like the Probation Service: they had both seen my potential, something I was unable to see myself, and both made me reach inside and pull it out. The thing I liked about Frank was that he was a man of principle: if he believed that something was right he would defend it to the hilt. Take his campaign to free Myra Hindley. He was totally blinkered to the public mood over the case. I had long conversations about it with him; I told him that no Home Secretary was ever going to release her — it would mean political suicide. But Frank believed that she was being unfairly treated by the criminal justice system. To some extent he had a point, but going and claiming in the media that she was "a good Catholic woman" did nothing to help his campaign to free her.

We would also have long conversations about equality, or equal opportunities, and nearly every time we discussed the topic, the Hindley case would come up. He would argue that there was inequality in the way she was being treated in prison, as it was different to the way other prisoners who had committed similar offences were treated. I would argue that her case was different, that she was the one who lured the children to Ian Brady so that he could murder them—she knew exactly what she was doing. With equality there has to be fairness: sure, she was being treated differently to other prisoners, but the majority of people in this country believed that it was fair that she remain in prison. In other words, she got her just desserts. Frank, on the other hand, wasn't bothered about public opinion; he said that two hundred years ago public opinion believed that slavery was a good thing. He was driven by his beliefs, which is a rare quality, and he continued to campaign for her release until his death in 2001.

Frank was also a very compassionate man. He would visit any prisoner who asked him to; he would zig-zag across the country sometimes doing so from one prison to another. There would be times when I had to visit the same prison as he did, in which case I would drive him there, we would see our respective prisoners, and then we would return home. Up until his death, Frank was visiting two prisons a week. He was truly "a friend of the friendless". Bernard Levin once wrote in *The Times* about Frank: "Everyone asks the wrong question about Lord Longford: Is he barmy? The question is not worth asking—of course he is barmy. What we should be discussing is something quite different: is he right? Of course he is right to stand up for what he perceived to be an injustice. Frank could never be accused of being a moral coward. He did not shy away from what he clearly believed was wrong. He was a latter-day David who tried to slay an insurmountable Goliath in the form of the media and public opinion, whilst I stood with some other metaphorical Israelites cheering him on from our hiding places."

I couldn't have said it better myself. Frank was truly a man of principle, and if that meant he would have to fly in the face of public opinion, so be it — he wasn't prepared to compromise those principles.

One of the fondest memories I have of him was when I walked into his office one day. He had his feet up on the desk and was reading *The Sun.* I said to him, "Why are you reading *that* paper?" He lowered it and said, "I have to see what the enemy is saying about me!"

Chapter 11

Life's most urgent question is:
"What are you doing for others?"

Martin Luther King

I recently went to a couple of meetings that I used to attend when I first got sober — they were still in the same venues. The Croydon meeting was the first one I ever went to. When I returned there I slipped into the back of the hall and took a seat; looking around there was no-one there that I knew. A young man came up to me and gave me a welcoming handshake; he introduced himself as Dave and asked if this was my first meeting. I said yes, well a least it was my first one that day!

The meeting got underway. The format was pretty much the same: someone opened the meeting and then introduced the person who was the main speaker for the evening. As I sat there looking around, I noticed that the room hadn't changed apart from a lick of paint. I started to think about all the people who had played a major part in my recovery: the Salvation Amy officer in Brixton Prison with her off-the-cuff remark that had pushed a button in my mind; the probation officer who didn't mince her words when it came to challenging me about my drinking and drug taking; Dr Gayford and his staff.

Pinel House, which was sadly demolished years ago along with Warlingham Park Hospital, is now a housing estate.

It was the salvation of many people like myself, but was closed in the late-1990s, the victim of government cuts. Without the help that was given to me in there, I wouldn't have survived.

As for the people I was in "the Group" with, I don't know what became of them. I have heard that some had relapsed; others had gone on to live successful lives. The people who were at the AA meetings when I first started to attend stretched out their hand of friendship to me, took me under their wings, and taught me by example how to stay away from that first drink one day at a time. Many of them have sadly died since, but their legacies live on. People like Harry, who took the time to make me feel welcome at my first meeting and was also the one who got me to speak at my first convention; he helped me take my first steps to becoming a public speaker. Then there was Lavatory Len: he used to always say that since I had stopped spewing over my own shoes, all my problems had become "high class". He showed me so much love and taught me how to be grateful for the life I was now leading. Every time I would walk into a meeting, if he was there, he would greet me with the same line: "What high class problems have you been struggling with today, Bob?" There were times that I could've gladly hit him, asking that same question over and over again; but of course he was right: now that I have stopped drinking and using, all my problems have become high class. All the major problems I wrestle with today are things like what clothes I should buy or which car I should drive, etc. etc.

Then there was little Irish Brendon. He never pulled any punches; he was the one who pointed out to me in a phone conversation that I was living in a nut house! One evening

I was chatting to him after a meeting and I told him that I was sick and tired of being in the rat race. He came back, quick as a flash, "Well stop being at rat then!" Brendon never used kid gloves when dealing with the newcomer; he did it because he loved people and he knew that we were dealing with a killer illness — straight talking was his way of tackling it. He was such a lovely man.

Then there were the real characters around the fellowship, people like Ironing Board Arthur, Big Michael, Old George, Commander Brian, and Racing Car John. These men had been sober for years and they would share their experiences, strength and hope with me. They were my role models; they were doing something positive with their lives and they were helping others along the way. It was these men who taught me the value of service. Working with others who were struggling with addiction made me realise that it was helping me to stay sober.

Also, women in the fellowship were great role models, like Lovely Margaret and Dinner Lady Lil. They were "lace curtain" drinkers: they would sit and drink at home where no-one could see them; to the outside world they were leading respectable lives, but they were suffering the exact same emotional pains as I was. They took the time to talk to someone like me, a former drug-crazed beggar. You could have mistakenly thought that these women and I had nothing in common, but we did: we were all alcoholics keeping away from that first drink, one day at a time.

Unlike some of the women I met, my drinking took me down a different path. A lot of it was done in the public gaze; my neighbours would give the police a standing ovation each time they came to arrest me! But what we had in common were those feelings of total despair that heavy drinking had brought us.

In my early days in the fellowship I was embarrassed about the fact that when I was drunk I would wet the bed — I never told a soul. Then one evening at a meeting a woman was in the chair and was telling her story. She told us that she was a bedwetter when drinking. By doing that she had given permission for me to talk about it too — I would wet the bed so often there would be a rainbow over it!

Recently, I found myself driving through Tooting in South London one Thursday evening. I looked to see if the meeting in that area was still going, and it was. It was years ago that I set-up that meeting because the place where we were currently meeting was closing. The venue I had selected was a church hall. The vicar who showed me round pointed out where the gents' toilets were; I had to ask about the ladies' — he thought that AA was a men's only club!

I dropped into the meeting. There was a whole new generation of people there. This time a young woman approached me and introduced herself as Sarah. She offered me a cup of tea or coffee; I said, "No thank you." She remarked that she hadn't seen me there before; I told her that I lived in Reading and was only passing through. She took me over and introduced me to a middle-aged man. I started chatting to him and he told me that he had stopped drinking three weeks ago. I thought to myself you are lucky, mate: when I was three weeks away from my last drink I wasn't able to get myself to meetings; I wasn't even allowed out on my own but had to be escorted by two male nurses so that I could walk from Pinel over to the main hospital to get a newspaper and some cigarettes. But this poor guy didn't know what day it was — the really silly thing was he thought that I did!

He asked how long I had been sober, but I skirted around his question. How could I tell him that my last drink was thirty years ago when he was just three weeks from his last one? I remember when I asked that question of Harry at my first meeting and he told me that he was five years sober — that blew me away!

I told him that I had been around for a bit, but that time doesn't really matter — it was just one day at a time. I sat next to him through the meeting. When it was finished, we went to the tea bar where there were other people talking. They got him involved in their conversation. He asked one of the guys how long this meeting had been here. Someone said they weren't quite sure but believed it started in the early-1980s. Then the conversation got round to who started it, but no-one knew. My ego wanted to say that it was me! I really struggled to keep my mouth shut because it wasn't about me — all I am is an ex-drunk trying to keep away from that first drink. If I were to drink tomorrow, the fellowship would go on without me. That is what it's all about, not my ego. I said "Goodnight," walked to my car and drove home.

Do I have any regrets about my life? Of course I do. Each time I committed a crime, there was a victim. I've been asked many times what made me turn my life around; I have a very simple answer to that question: I stopped feeling sorry for myself and started to feel sorry for other people, especially my victims.

For almost all of the time that I've been clean and sober, I have tried to work with victims of crime; my work has always been driven with them in mind. When I think about the amount of misery I must have inflicted on other people, I feel a deep sense of shame. I would do my best to dehumanise my victims: if I broke into someone's home, I wouldn't look at the family photos because that meant that they were real people. I just wanted to steal inanimate objects to feed my unquenchable habit for alcohol and pills.

When an offence is committed it is seen to be committed against the state, and the victim and offender rarely if ever meet. In some instances the victim's case is not even acknowledge in court; their offences get lost in the list of offences taken into consideration (TICs) when an offender is being sentenced, robbing victims of their day in court — how frustrating this can be to the poor victim.

When I was offending I had no responsibility to my victims. I was sent to prison where I would feel sorry for *myself*. It's only when the offender pleads "not guilty" that the victim may get to go to court to give evidence at the trial; then they run the chance of being victimised all over again in the cross-examination. A lot of offenders will plead guilty, which they usually do to avoid a longer sentence — it's all part of a tactical game in which the only thing that matters is when they will get back out on the streets again.

In this, there doesn't seem to be any fairness. When I would talk to an offender about their sentences, in almost every case they would tell me that they were too harsh for what they had done. And yet, on the other hand, when I asked the victim what they thought about the sentence given to the offender, most of them would say that it was not enough. Even with the severest punishment, crime can leave unresolved issues that lie dormant in the mind of a victim for years. During one of the radio phone-ins I've been involved in, one caller told me he had been burgled twenty years earlier, but he and his family were still reliving the experience; even after all this time they were still searching around car-boot sales and charity shops in the hope that they might one day find his late grandmother's wedding ring. The family had not been able to have "closure".

The existing system breeds conflict. Questions remain unanswered and the victim cannot move on. His or her sense of security is shattered, and victims have a tendency to blame themselves for what happened. They relive the crime in their minds over-and-over-again and they can remain in that state for decades. Perhaps the reason why so many people line up to appear in audience discussion programmes on television is so that they can at last vent their anger and get it off their chests.

There is, however, a way that the victim can play an active and positive role: this is through restorative justice. Restorative justice is a concept which promotes repairing the overall damage that crime has caused to people. It is when the victim and the offender *are* brought together. The offender doesn't tell the victim *how* they did it, but *why* they did; in return the victim tells the offender the impact that their offending has had on him or her. As a probation officer, I have sat in on many Restorative Conferences, both in prison and in the community. I have witnessed offenders reduced to tears after hearing the impact their offending has had on other people. The victim is able to bring closure to the offence and then they can move on. I know, without a doubt, that if I had been confronted with one of my own victims, it would have stopped me dead in my tracks.

What makes someone like me turn away from a lifestyle that was self-indulgent and often self-destructive? I'm asked to give presentations to universities, colleges and prisons talking about my life experiences. I find many people who believe that I managed to turn my life around because of willpower; however, willpower alone does not work. Try applying willpower to keeping your eyes open when you sneeze — it doesn't work. The desire to drink or take a drug is so overwhelming; it's like swimming under water: when a swimmer is out of breath, the compulsion to swim to the surface is so strong that nothing is going to stop him or her from doing so. That is what it's like when that compulsion hits the addict within us — willpower alone will not be enough.

For years I have worked with people who have been addicted to alcohol and drugs. I have found that they need to undergo a paradigm shift, a complete change in their perception and understanding of the world around them. Paradigms are formed by the way we see ourselves and they can do so at a very early age. They are like maps in our heads. Just as we could never find our way around London if we were using a map of Paris, so with the wrong paradigm in our heads we are not going to be able to negotiate ourselves through life in a constructive way.

In my case, I saw myself for many years as not being good enough and likewise I behaved as if I wasn't good enough. And of course I would behave in a negative way to the challenges I came across. It was when I was in Pinel that I had my own epiphany or paradigm shift. I called Pinel a "paradigm factory": when I was in the Group I had light bulb moments all the time, each made up of little paradigm shifts.

In my opinion there are three levels of motivation: the first level is the social one, when the addict comes under pressure from their family and friends to stop their using. That might have an effect in the short term, but always they will return to those old patterns of behaviour. The next level is the fear of public judgment — the fear of being arrested, appearing in court or even going to prison — that will stop some people for a while; but again they will always return to negative patterns of behaviour. Then there is the top level of motivation where the person *chooses* not to drink or not to take drugs. This is when they make a decision independently of any other influences around them or what people think of them, a decision that they need to stop drinking and using for themselves — in other words, when they have a paradigm shift.

What happens to those people who don't reach the third level of motivation? Addiction is a dangerous disease that if left unchecked can destroy them. In many of these cases the sufferer has actually died prematurely; but in others the body has lived on but in quiet desperation, without hope and, in many cases, without the support of family or friends. We are quick to judge sometimes the relatives or loved ones of the addict for "abandoning" the person; but distancing themselves from their loved ones, whether geographically or emotionally, can often be the only way the family can survive. I have also seen the opposite, where family or friends can create a "dependency culture" and actually enable addicts to continue to destroy themselves by never letting them face the consequences of their actions. Due to my deep Christian faith, I believe most people are not beyond hope.

Another regret I have is that I didn't have a youth. It was either spent in prison or drunk. Our early years should be a time of enjoyment; a time to discover the world around us; a time to build friendships that will endure for years. I had none of those experiences. You can determine the kind of life you will have in your thirties and forties by what you do in your teenage years. We only get one shot at this life and this is not a dress rehearsal.

Everything I have today is a gift. Sometimes I really do need reminding just how greatly blessed I am. When I am feeling discontented with life, this is when I throw myself into the service of others, working with someone who is having problems with alcohol or drug abuse, or trying to bring comfort to the parents of a wayward child.

I have also been blessed with a wonderful wife. I never felt that it would be possible for me to have a relationship with someone on the level that I have with Sue. Of all the people in my life, she has been the most significant influence. She is a great example to me; she has taught me so much. I have never known anyone quite like her. Her level of understanding is unfathomable. I have watched her in wonderment as she has mothered our children and have greatly admired the relationship she has with them; now she is doing the same with our grandchildren. She has a very special spirit about her. Without a doubt I have married above myself! People have asked me what my greatest talent is; I reply that, as I've mentioned before in this book, the only talent I have is that I can choose a good wife!

I often jokingly ask her, "When you first walked into that room in Pinel House and saw me sitting there, wasted away through years of alcohol and drug abuse, wrists in bandages from a suicide attempt, surely you must of thought to yourself, 'That's my future husband sitting there'?" I feel a great sense of gratitude that she has chosen someone like me to be her friend and companion. I must have done something right somewhere to have someone as wonderful as Sue by my side.

Looking back on our journey together, now that the kids are grown up and have kids of their own, I recognise that it has by no means been plain sailing all the way. Family life is not perfect and a couple of our children have made decisions that have concerned us. I think that one of the most difficult things in becoming a parent of adult children is when you become a spectator in your children's lives and watch them make their own mistakes. However, none of them are making the grave mistakes continuously that I did when I was their age. Today I try not to make the same mistakes that I did in the past.

As for my brothers, ten years after my brother Fred died, my older brother Stan was very ill. The year before his wife had died of cancer. They had no children. Stan was sixteen years older than me and went into the army when he was eighteen. After twenty years service, he and his wife set up home in Taunton, Somerset. Shortly following his wife's death, he became unwell. I spent the last day of his life with him in the hospital; at the end I was holding him in my arms and stroking his forehead. He died peacefully in my arms — there is something very intimate about being with someone in the last moments of their life.

As for my brother Tom, he followed me into the fellowship and has been sober for over twenty years. Both he and his wife still do a lot of good for the organization.

My gratitude overwhelms me. No matter how many talks I do in prisons, no matter how many lost souls I try to reach in meetings, if I spend the rest of my life doing these things it would not even begin to repay a small part of what has been done for me. On a lighter note I was recently in a book shop and on the shelves were copies of one of my books. I thought to myself, "Not bad for The Idiot Boy!"

THE END

You can follow Bob on:
Twitter: @bobturney
Facebook: Bob Turney
www.bobturney.com

So You Think You Know Me?
by Allan Weaver
With a Foreword by Mike Nellis and Fergus McNeill

The autobiography of an ex-offender and twice-times inmate of Barlinnie Prison, now a social work team-leader in his native Scotland. As a local hard case, author Allan Weaver took no prisoners. Neither does he in this compelling work in which he tells of violent episodes and his chaotic early life. Essential reading for anyone involved with serious young offenders, especially those of a violent disposition.

'When Mr Weaver talks about the importance of tackling the causes of crime, he does so from an unusual position of authority and experience': *The Scotsman*

Paperback & Ebook | ISBN 978-1-904380-45-0 | 2008 | 224 pages

www.WatersidePress.co.uk

The Little Book Of Prison
A Beginners Guide
Frankie Owens

The Little Book of Prison: A Beginners Guide
by Frankie Owens

Koestler Platinum Award Winning guide to prison. An easy-to-read prison survival guide of do's and don'ts. Perfect for anyone facing trial for an offence that may lead to imprisonment, their families and friends. Packed with humour as well as more serious items. Backed by prisoner support organizations. Straightforward and highly entertaining.

'By the end of the book, I felt like Frankie Owens was my cell-mate. His style and execution is either perversely skilful or an absolute fluke, but whatever it is, it is certainly good':
Prison Service Journal

Paperback & Ebook | ISBN 978-1-90438-083-2 | 2012 | 112 pages

www.WatersidePress.co.uk

Going Straight: After Crime and Punishment
by Angela Devlin and Bob Turney
With a Foreword by Jack Straw

Going Straight looks at a range of offenders who have changed their way of life. They include famous, notorious, creative and ordinary people who were prepared to talk about the turning point in their lives—the events which caused them to leave crime behind.

Paperback & Ebook | ISBN 978-1-872870-66-3 | 1999 | 272 pages

www.WatersidePress.co.uk

Letters to a Lifer: The Boy 'Never to be Released'
by Cindy Sanford
With a Foreword by Jeanne Bishop

Letters to a Lifer provides a rare insight into life without parole (LWOP) for juveniles in the USA. A true story from Pennsylvania, it is a compelling tale of faith and redemption. Cindy Sanford tells how a chance correspondence with Ken, a prisoner artist, began to change her entrenched ideas about offenders. Her book now adds voice to the work of the USA's National Campaign for the Fair Sentencing of Youth and will also be of interest to students of restorative justice.

Paperback & Ebook | ISBN 978-1-909976-15-3 | 2015 | 240 pages

www.WatersidePress.co.uk

The Lost Boyz: A Dark Side of Graffiti
by Justin Rollins
With a Foreword by Noel 'Razor' Smith

A rare first-hand account of disaffected youth. Contains countless lessons for young people who might be attracted to crime (and anyone involved with them socially or professionally).

'This is simply 100% raw talent being unleashed right from the start... This book is a must-read for the prison population, academics and politicians':
Inside Time

Paperback & Ebook | ISBN 978-1-904380-67-2 | 2011 | 176 pages

www.WatersidePress.co.uk

Lightning Source UK Ltd.
Milton Keynes UK
UKOW06f1320171115

262924UK00001B/3/P

9 781909 976252